DICTIO____ ____
OF
FRENCH
BUILDING
TERMS

Essential for renovators,
builders and home-owners

FRENCH–ENGLISH
ENGLISH–FRENCH

Edited by Richard Wiles

summersdale

DICTIONARY OF BUILDING TERMS

Text by Richard Wiles

Summersdale Publishers Ltd
46 West Street
Chichester
West Sussex
PO19 1RP
UK

www.summersdale.com

Printed and bound in Great Britain

ISBN 1 84024 494 1

ISBN 13: 978 1 84024 494 6

Thanks to my niece Hollie Wiles for her invaluable
assistance in the compilation of this book, and to my
brother Phill Wiles for additional expertise.

Other research was carried out with
the assistance of the following websites:

www.pointp.fr
www.castorma.fr
www.leroymerlin.fr
www.ideesmaison.fr
www.outilex.com
www.menuiserie-caserotto.com
www.mr-bricolage.fr
www.tout-faire.com
www.screwfix.com
www.tool-net.co.uk
www.toolfinder.co.uk

Contents

FRENCH–ENGLISH

BUILDING

MAÇONNERIE

CONSTRUCTION
ROOFING
INSULATION
DAMP-PROOFING
PLASTERING
DRAINAGE

absorb, to absorber *v*

abut, to abouter *v*

accelerator accélérateur *m*

access aperture for cleaning (e.g. soot box) orifice de ramonage *m*

accessory accessoire *m*

additive adjuvant *m*; additif *m*

additive, concrete anti-freeze adjuvant pour bétonnage par temps froid *m*

additive, mortar and concrete adjuvant des mortiers *m*

additive, mortar and concrete cold temperature accelerator adjuvant accélérateur antigel *m*

additive, mortar and concrete plasticiser adjuvant plastifiant *m*

additive, mortar and concrete reinforcing adjuvant fibres synthétiques *m*

additive, mortar and concrete water repellent adjuvant hydrofuge *m*

adhere, to adhérer *v*

adhesion adhérence *f*

adhesive, insulating materials colle matériaux d'isolation *f*

adhesive, neoprene colle néoprène *f*

adhesive, plaster block colle à carreau de plâtre *f*

adhesive, waterproof colle hydro *f*

adjustable support étai réglable *m*

against the grain (wood) contre-fil *adj*

aggregate agrégat *m*

aggregate, polystyrene polystyrène adjuvanté *m*

air bubble layer (aluminium insulator) film à bulle d'air sec *m*

air compressor compresseur d'air *m*

air gap (cavity wall) couche d'air *f*

air grille grille d'aeration *f*

air inlet prise d'air *f*

air vent (of fireplace) ventouse *f*

alcove alcôve *f*

align, to aligner *v*

aluminium film layer, exterior isolation film éxterieur réflecteur alu *m*

aluminium foil reflective insulator isolant mince alu réfléchissant *m*

aluminium insulation air bubble layer isolation film à bulle d'air sec *m*

anchor ancre *f*

anchor/fix, to ancrer *v*

ancient ancien -enne *adj*

angle bead bourrelet d'étanchéité *m*; éclisse cornière *f*; baguette d'angle *f*

angle grinder meuleuse d'angle *f*

angle iron cornière *f*; fer d'angle *m*

annexe annexe *f*

anti-backflow throat (fireplace) gorge anti-refoulante *f*

anti-humidity anti-humidité *adj*

anti-moss masonry treatment, colourless traitement incolore antimousse *m*

antirust antirouille *adj*

apartment appartement *m*; logement *m*

aperture orifice *m*

appliance appareil *m*

arch voûte *f*

arch pillar trumeau *m (see also: overmantel)*

architect architecte *m*

architrave architrave *f*; baguette *f*

asbestos free sans amiante *adj*

assemble, to assembler *v*

assessment bilan *m*

avoid, to éviter *v*

awl alêne *f*

axe hache *f*

back arrière *m*

back door porte de derrière *f*

balcony balcon *m*

ball-socket cuvette rotule *f*

ballast blocaille *f*; granulat *m*

baluster, staircase balustre *m*

balustrade balustrade *f*

banister (handrail) rampe *f*

bars (window); grille grille *f*

base base *f*; fondation *f*

base-board plinthe *f*

basement sous-sol *m*

basic structure gros oeuvre *m*

batten liteau *m*

beam poutre *f*; poutrelle *f*

beam, exposed poutre apparente *f*

beam, large wooden madrier *m*

beam, prestressed concrete poutre précontrainte *f*; poutrelle céramique *f*; poutrelle béton *f*

beam, prestressed flooring
plancher précontraint *m*
bearer support *m*
bed of concrete lit de béton *m*
bend coude *m*
bend, to cintrer *v*
bevel biseau *m*
**bevel, adjustable/sliding/
combination** fausse équerre *f*
bevel, to biseauter *v*
bevelled biseauté -e *adj*; en biseau
bind, to lier *v*
binding material liant *m*
bitumen bitume *m*
bituminous liquid revêtement
bitumineux *m*
blade lame *f*
**block, cellular terracotta
insulating** brique auto-
isolante en terre cuite *f*
**block, concrete cellular
insulating** bloc béton
cellulaire *m*
**block, decorative concrete
walling** muret béton décoratif *m*
block, foundation massif de
fondation *m*
block, hollow concrete bloc
creux en béton *m*
block, lintel bloc linteau *m*

block pillar, walling pilier *m*
**block, reconstituted stone
walling** muret pierre
reconstituée *m*
block, solid aggregate bloc
plein de granulats *m*
block, solid concrete bloc
plein en béton *m*
block up, to reboucher *v*
blockage obstruction *f*;
blocage *m*
board, skirting plinthe *f*
boarding planchéiage *m*
bolt boulon *m*
bolt cutters coupe-boulons *m*
**bonding beam/girder
(reinforcement)** chaînage *m*
border bord *m*
botch, to bâcler *v*; gâcher *v*
boundary fence clôture de
bornage *f*
boundary stone or marker
borne *f*
boxing, housing
emboîtement *m*
brace raidisseur *m*; entretoise *f*
brace (of truss) contrefiche *f*
brace (timber frame) écharpe *f*
breadth largeur *m*
breezeblock parpaing *m*

breezeblock, alleviated bloc
plein allégé *m*

breezeblock, full size bloc
plein *m*

**breezeblock, hollow (for
filling with concrete)** bloc
creux *m*; ~ à bancher *m*

**breezeblock, perforated full
size** bloc plein perforé *m*

**breezeblock, pilaster (for
reinforcement)** bloc
d'angle *m*

breezeblock, thin profile
planelle *f*

**breezeblock, thin profile
hollow** planelle perforée *f*

**breezeblock, U-shaped
channel** bloc U *m*

brick brique *f*

brick, arch brique à couteau *f*

brick, facing (or facing block)
plaquette de parement *f*

brick, full size brique pleine *f*

brick, glass brique de verre *f*

brick, half-width mulot *m*

brick, hollow terracotta
brique creuse de terre cuite *f*

brick jointer fer à joint plat *m*

brick-paved pavé -e de brique
adj

brick paving carrelage en
briques *m*

brick, perforated brique
perforée *f*

brick, standard type brique de
type courant *f*

brick, to briqueter *v*; maçonner
v; murer *v*

brick, ventilation brique de
ventilation *f*

brick up, to maçonner *v*

broom balai *m*

brush brosse *f*

bucket, builder's seau (*pl* -x) de
maçon *m*

build, to bâtir *v*; construire *v*

building bâtiment *m*

building land terrain
constructible *m*

building permit permis de
construire *m*

building site chantier *m*

building stone moellon *m*

bulge, to (e.g. wall) bomber *v*

cable câble *m*

cable, buried câble enterré *m*

cantilever encorbellement *m*

capacity (e.g. of reservoir)
contenance *f*

caulker couteau (*pl* -x) à enduire *m*

caving in éboulement *m*;
  effondrement *m*

cavity cavité *f*; trémie *f*

ceiling plafond *m*

ceiling, false faux plafond *f*

cellar cave *m*

cement ciment *m*

cement, all-purpose ciment
  multi-usages *m*

cement, dry-mixed ciment prêt
  à l'emploi *m*

cement, extra-white ciment
  super blanc *m*

cement, grey ciment gris *m*; **(all-purpose)** ~ multi-usages *m*

cement, heat-resistant ciment
  fondu *m*

cement, high-performance
  ciment hautes performances *m*

cement/lime mix bâtard
  mortier *m*

cement, masonry ciment à
  maçonner *m*

cement mixer bétonnière *f*;
  bétonneuse *f*

cement, quick-setting ciment
  prompt *m*; ~ bâti prompt *m*

cement, sack of sac de ciment *m*

cement, special-purpose
  ciment spécial *m*

cement, sulphate-resisting
  ciment milieux aggressifs *m*

cement, tile joint ciment
  joint *m*

cement, to cimenter *v*;
  bétonner *v*

cement, white ciment blanc *m*;
  (all-purpose) ~ multi-usages *m*

cesspool fosse d'aisance *f*

chalk poudre à tracer *f*; craie *f*

chimney cheminée *f*

chimney cap chapeau de
  cheminée *m*

**chimney flaunching,
  preformed** embase
  d'étanchéité cheminée *f*

chimney flue conduit de
  cheminée *m*

chimney flue, aluminium
  conduit de cheminée en
  aluminium *m*

chimney flue extractor
  extracteur éolien *m*; aspirateur
  dynamique éolien *m*

chimney flue, insulated
  conduit de cheminée isolé *m*

chimney flue liner, flexible
  tubage de conduit flexible *m*

chimney flue, stainless steel
  conduit de cheminée en inox *m*

chimney opening trémie de cheminée *f*

chimney panel panneau de cheminée *m*

chimney stack, prefabricated sortie de toit *f*

chimney, terracotta block conduit de fumée en terre cuite *m*

chipboard panneau de particules *m*; aggloméré (*abbr:* agglo) *m*

chisel -s ciseau (*pl* -x) *m*

chisel, bolster ciseau à brique *m*

chisel, cold ciseau de maçon *m*

chisel, chasing chasse à pierre *f*

chisel, masonry pointerolle de maçon *f*

chisel, plugging no equivalent (*nearest see: masonry chisel*)

chisel, protective hand grip for poignée pare-coup *f*

chisel, to ciseler *v*

cistern citerne *f*; réservoir d'eau *m*

cladding lambris *m*; revêtement *m*

clamp agrafe *f*; bride *f*

clamp, to serrer *v*; brider *v*; cramponner *v*

clamp, mason's serre-joint de maçon *m*

clamping peg chevillette *f*

clay argile *f*

clean down, to (brickwork) ragréer *v*

clear, to vider *v*

coat, finishing (e.g. plaster) couche de finition *f*

coating (e.g. plaster) enduit *m*

coating of fill-in material (e.g. plaster, mortar) solin *m*

coating, waterproof revêtement imperméable *m*

cobblestone pavé *m*

colourant colorant *m*

colourant, concrete and mortar colorant béton et mortier *m*

colourant, iron oxide colorant oxyde de fer *m*

colourant, powder colorant en poudre *m*

combine, to mêler *v*; combiner *v*

compact, to compacter *v*

concrete béton *m*

concrete air entraining agent agent entraîneur d'air *m*

concrete, lightweight béton allégé libre *m*

concrete mix mélange béton *m*

concrete mould release agent décoffrant démoulage *m*

concrete, rapid-setting béton à prise rapide *m*

concrete repairer/restorer réparation béton *f*

concrete set retarder retardateur de prise pour béton *m*

concrete surface hardener durcisseur de surface fixateur *m*

connecting to the drains raccordement aux égouts *m*

construction fault/damage dommage-ouvrage *m*

contract contrat *m*

contraction rétrécissement *m*

contractor entrepreneur *m*

control réglementation *f*

conversion aménagement *m*

convert, to aménager *v*

convert into, to convertir en *v*

cooling-off period délai de réflexion *m*

cork insulating underlay (tiles) sous-couche liège isol carrelage *f*

cork soundproofing underlay (floors) sous-couche liège sol isolation phonique *f*

corrugated roof panel plaque ondulée *f*

council offices mairie *f*

counter compteur *m*

courtyard cour *f*

courtyard, inner cour intérieure *f*

cove corniche *f*

cover (e.g. inspection chamber) couvercle *m*

cover, to couvrir *v*

coving corniche *f*

crack fissure *f*

crevice lézarde *f*

cross-bar traverse *f*

crowbar pied-de-biche *m*

crush, to concasser *v*

cubic metre mètre en cube *m*

cupboard, built-in placard *m*

curve cintre *m*

curve, to cintrer *v*

cut, to couper *v*

cutting disc, diamond disque diamante *m*

damp-proof imperméable *adj*

damp-proof course couche isolant *f*

damp-proof membrane protection soubassement *f*; pare-vapeur kraft *m*

deadline délai *m*

debris décombres *mpl*

defect défaut *m*

delay délai *m*

delivery date délai de livraison *m*

demolish, to démolir *v*

density densité *f*

depth profondeur *m*

design dessin *m*

develop, to aménager *v*

development (progress) déroulement *m*

diameter diamètre *m*

dig, to creuser *v*

dividing wall cloison de distribution *f*

dormer window truss fermette *f (see also: false gable)*

double glazing double vitrage *f*

downpipe (guttering) tuyau de descente *m*

drain clearing kit kit de débouchage *m*

drain, to vider *v;* égoutter *v*

drainage drainage *m*

drainage channel caniveau en béton *m*

drainage channel, concrete caniveau en béton *m*

drainage channel, glass reinforced plastic caniveau polyester renforcé de fibre de verre *m*

drainage ditch fossé collecteur *m*

drainpipe tube de drainage *m;* ~ d'assainissement *m*

drainpipe, land drain agricole *m*

draw, to tracer *v;* dessiner *v*

draw plans, to tirer des plans *v*

drawing dessin *m;* plan *m*

drill perceuse *f*

drill bit mèche *f;* foret *m*

drill bit, auger mèche à spiral unique *f*

drill bit, expansive mèche à bois extensible *f*

drill bit, flat mèche à bois plate *f*

drill bit, glass/ceramic/ porcelain mèche à ogive/au carbure/de tungstène *f*

drill bit, masonry foret à béton *m*

drill bit, metal foret à metaux *m*

drill bits, set of coffret de forets/mèches *m*

drill bit, twist mèche hélicoidale *f*

drill bit, wood mèche à bois *f*

drill, corded percussion perceuse à percussion filaire *f*

drill, cordless percussion perceuse à percussion sans fil *f*

drill, demolition marteau démolisseur *m*; ~ piqueur *m*

drill, hammer (with or without cord) marteau perforateur *m*

drill, pneumatic hammer perforateur électropneumatique *m*

drill/screwdriver perceuse visseuse *f*

drill, to forer *v* (a hole); percer *v* (a hole in a board)

drop chute *f*

dry rot pourriture sèche *f*

duct conduite *f*

dump, to déposer *v*

dust poussière *f*

eaves avant-toit extérieur *m*; comble extérieur *m*

eaves crawlspace combles perdus *mpl*

edge beam (e.g. wall plate) poutre de rive *f*

edifice édifice *m*

elevation élévation *f*

empty vide *adj*

empty, to vider *v*

empty out, to vidanger *v*

empty space vide *m*

enclosure clôture *f*

end (work), to achever *v*

engineer ingénieur *m*

enlarge, to agrandir *v*

entrance entrée *f*

entry entrée *f*

estimate devis *m*

estimate (quantities/costs) métré *m*

exit dégagement *m*

expand, to dilater *v*

expanded clay argile expansée *f*

expanded polystyrene polystyrène expansé *m*

expanding polyurethane foam filler mousse expansive polyuréthane *f*

extension agrandissement *m*

exterior extérieur *m*

extruded polystyrene polystyrène extrudé *m*

extruded polystyrene board, groove-edged polystyrène extrudé bord rainuré *m*

extruded polystyrene board, square-edged polystyrène extrudé bord droit *m*

face (e.g. of a rock) paroi *f*

facilities équipements *mpl*

false gable fermette *f*

fan ventilateur *m*

fan, electric ventilateur électrique *m*

fan, extractor ventilateur extracteur *m*

fascia panneau *m*

fence, concrete clôture en béton *f*

file lime *f*

filer, electric lime électrique *f*

fill, to remblayer *v*

fill a crack, to reboucher *v*

filler enduit *m*

filler, fine joint enduit poudre de collage et finition *m*

filler, fine-surface enduit de lissage *m*

filler, finishing enduit de finition *m*

filler, high quality enduit surfin *m*

filler, jointing enduit à joint *m*

filler, pre-mixed enduit prêt à l'emploi *m*

filler, quick-setting enduit à prise rapide *m*; **(joint)** ~ poudre à prise rapide *m*

filler, ready-to-use enduit à joint prêt à l'emploi *m*

filler, repair enduit de rebouchage *m*

filler, slow-drying enduit à joint prise lente *m*

filler, waterproof enduit d'étanchéité *m*

fireplace cheminée *f*

fireplace insert insert de cheminée *m*

fire-proof ignifuge *adj*

fire resistance résistance au feu *f*

first floor premier étage *m*

fishpond réservoir bassin *m*

fit, to équiper *v*

fix, to ancrer *v*

flagstone pavé *m*

flange collet *m*

flashing strip bande d'étanchéité *f*; ~ de solin *f (see also: flaunching)*

flashing strip, self-adhesive tear-resistant bande d'étanchéité indéchirable autocollante *f*

flaunching bande de solin *f (see also: flashing)*

flaunching, roof ridge/hip rafter closoir de faîtage et de arêtier *m*

flight of stairs rampe d'escalier *f*

float, foam taloche polystyrène *f*

float, plasterer's taloche *f*

float, plastic taloche plastique *f*

float, steel platroir à enduire inoxidable *m*

float, wooden taloche bois *f*

floor; flooring plancher *m*; sol *m*

floor batten lambourde *f*

floorboard planche *f*

foam rubber mousse expansée *f*

formwork coffrage *m*

formwork clamp serre-joint de cimentier *m*

foundation trench rigole *f*

foundations fondations *fpl*

frame, door or window chambranle *m*

framework charpente *f*

gable pignon *m*

gas gaz *m*

gas supply alimentation en gaz *f*

gate porte *f*

generator groupe électrogène *m*

girder poutre en fer *f (see also: RSJ)*

glass fibre fibres de verre *f*

glass wool laine de verre *f*

glass wool, roll rouleau de laine de verre *m*

grating, galvanised metal grille caillebotis en acier galvanisé *f*

gravel gravillon *m*; gravier *m*

gravel, bulk quantity gravillon en vrac *m*

gravel, fine non-rolled mignonnette non roulée *f*

gravel, rolled gravillon roulé *m*

grease trap (for drainage system) bac dégraisseur *m*

grille (e.g. inspection chamber) grille *f*

groove rainure *f*

groove, to rainurer *v*

ground sol *m*; terre *f*

ground floor rez-de-chaussée *m*

grout mortier *m*

gully, rainwater regard de branchement pour eaux pluviales *m*

gutter gouttière *f*

gutter board planche de rive *f*

gypsum gypse *m*

gypsum board plaque de gypse *f*
gypsum, fibre reinforced
gypse renforcé fibre *f*
hacksaw scie à métaux *f*
half-brick demi-brique *f*
half-timbering (typical of
Normandy) colombage *m*
hammer -s marteau (*pl* -x) *m*
hammer, brick marteau à briques *m*
hammer, claw marteau arrache-
clou *m*
hammer, club/lump massette *f*;
marteau de maçon *m*
hammer, lath/drywall hachette
de plâtrier *f*
hammer, packer's (claw
hammer) marteau d'emballeur
m; ~ de coffreur *m*
hammer, sculptor's (for
dressing concrete,
marble, granite) marteau à
boucharder *m*
hammer, sledge masse couple *f*
hammer, small (esp slater's)
martelette *f*
hardware quincaillerie *f*
hatchet hachette *f*
hawk, plasterer's taloche *f (see*
also: float, plasterer's)
hearth foyer *m*

hemp wool laine de chanvre *f*
hessian toile de jute *f*
high pressure cleaner
nettoyeur haute pression *m*
hipped roof, side of a rive
latérale *f*
hipped roof, top side of a rive
de tête *f*
hole ouverture *f*; trou *m*
hole saw scie-cloche *f*
hot-air gun décapeur
thermique *m*
house maison *f*
inspection chamber,
concrete (with cover or
grill) regard béton (avec
couvercle ou grille) *m*
insulating cork underlay
(fitted carpet) sous-couche
liège isol moquette *f*
insulating mastic (doors and
windows) mastic isolation
portes-fenêtres *m*
insulating material isolant *m*
insulation, intermediate
film layer film réflecteur
intermédiaire *m*
insulation kit (garage door)
kit d'isolation pour porte de
garage *m*

insulation kit (woodwork) kit d'isolation de menuiseries *m*

insulation, outer aluminium film layer film extérieur réflecteur alu *m*

insulation, sound, soundproofing isolation phonique *f*; ~ acoustique *f*

insulation suspension clip suspente pour laine de verre *f*

insulation, tear-resistant reflective membrane film armé réflecteur résistant à la déchirure *m*

insulation, thermal/heat isolation thermique *m*

intermediate film layer (insulation) isolation film réflecteur intermédiare *m*

ironwork ferraillage *m*

jamb jambage *m*

join, to assembler *v*

joiner menuisier *m*

joint assemblage *m*

joist solive *f*

joist hanger sabot de poutre *f*

keyed joint assemblage à clés amovibles *m*

labour main-d'œuvre *f*

labourer travailleur *m*

ladder échelle *f*

lagging calorifugeage *m*

landing, staircase palier *m*

lath latte *f*; volige *f*

lay, to poser *v*

layer couche *f*

layer, protective polypropylene voile protecteur en polypropylène *f*

lean-to appentis *m*

level -s niveau (*pl* -x) *m*

level, laser niveau laser *m*

level, spirit niveau à bulle *m*

lever levier *m*

lime chaux *f*

lime, coloured chaux colorée teintée *f*

lime, grey chaux grise *f*

lime, hydraulic chaux hydraulique *f*

lime, naturally formulated chaux naturelle formulae *f*

lime, natural white chaux blanche naturelle *f*

lime paint badigeon *m (see also: whitewash)*

lime, St. Astier chaux de Saint Astier *f*

limestone pierre calcaire *f*

lining doublage *m*; revêtement *m*

lining material matériaux de revêtement *m*

lintel -s linteau (*pl* -x) *m*

lintel, prestressed concrete prelinteau précontraint *m*

liquid waterproofer hydrofuge liquide *m*

loft grenier *m*

lower, to surbaisser *v*

machinery appareil *m*

manhole regard d'assainissement *m*; ~ de drainage *m*; trappe de visite *f*

manhole cover plaque d'égout *f*

marble marbre *m*

masonry treatment, colourless anti-moss traitement incolore antimousse *m*

masonry treatment, colourless water repellant traitement incolore imperméabilisant *m*

masonry treatment, exterior traitement façades murs extérieurs *m*

mattock pioche de cantonnier *f*

measure mesure *f*

measure, laser télémètre laser *m*

measure, retractable tape mesure roulante *f*

metal frame (partition wall) ossature métallique *f*

metal rail (partition wall) rail métallique *m*

meter, electricity/water compteur *m*

metre mètre *m*

mix, to (e.g. concrete) mélanger *v*

mixing attachment (for drill) malaxeur portif *m*

mix together, to mêler *v*; combiner *v*

mortar mortier *m*

mortar, coloured mortier coloré *m*; **(brick red)** ~ rouge brique *m*; **(dark beige)** ~ beige foncé *m*; **(dark grey)** ~ gris profond *m*; **(pink amber)** ~ rose ambre *m*

mortar, dry-mixed mortier prêt à l'emploi *m*

mortar, fine mortier fin *m*

mortar, finishing and smoothing mortier de ragréage et de lissage *m*

mortar, fine white mortier fin blanc *m*

mortar, grey mortier gris *m*

mortar, grey ready-mixed pointing mortier prêt mix jointoiement gris *m*

mortar, grey repair mortier de réparation gris *m*

mortar, lime bâtard mortier *m*

mortar, pointing mortier de jointoiement *m*

mortar, quick-setting mortier rapide *m*; ~ à prise rapide *m*

mortar, refractory heat-resistant mortier réfractaire *m*

mortar, repair mortier de réparation *m*

mortar, waterproofing mortier d'imperméabilisation *m*

mortar, white mortier blanc *m*

mud boue *f*

mullion -s meneau (*pl* -x) *m*

newel post, staircase noyau d'escalier *m*

nosing (e.g. of a stair tread) bord arrondi *m*

overmantel trumeau *m* (*see also: arch pillar*)

panel panneau *m*

panelling boiserie *f*; lambris *m*

pantile; roman tile tuile canal *f*

partition wall cloison *f*

partition, vertical paroi verticale *f*

patio terrasse *f*

paved pavé, -e *adj*

paving dallage *m*; pavage *m*

paving brick brique de pavage *f*

paving edging bordurette *f*

paving stone dalle *f*

pebbledash cailloutage *m*

pick pioche *f*

pick axe pioche hache *f*; ~ de terrassier *f*

pigment, natural pigment naturel *m*; (**sienna**) ~ terre de sienne *m*; (**umber**) ~ terre d'ombre *m*; (**yellow ochre**) ~ ocre jaune *m*

pillar colonne *f*

pillar, walling bloc pilier *m*

placing, installation pose *f*

plane rabot *m*

plaster plâtre *m*

plaster, alleviated plâtre allégé *m*

plaster, backing plâtre manuel gros *m*

plaster bead, galvanised aluminium protège angle galvanisé *m*

plaster block carreau plâtre *m*

plaster block, hollow carreau de plâtre creux *m*

plaster block, honeycomb carreau alvéolé *m*

plaster block, solid carreau plein *m*

plaster block, waterproofed carreau de plâtre hydrofugé *m*

plaster, board finish no equivalent in France

plaster, bonding (undercoat for low suction background/concrete/plasterboard)

plaster, browning (undercoat for solid background/moderate suction)

plaster, casting plâtre prestia *m*

plaster, fine white plâtre fin blanc *m*

plaster, fire-resistant plâtre incendie *m*

plaster, hand-mixing plâtre manuel *m*

plaster, moulding plâtre à modeler *m*

plaster, multi-finish no equivalent in France

plaster of Paris plâtre de Paris *m*

plaster, powder plâtre en poudre *m*

plaster, projection plâtre à projecter *m*

plaster, to plâtrer *v*

plaster, universal/multi-finish plâtre multi-usage *m*

plaster, pumice plâtre ponce *m*

plasterboard plaque de plâtre *f*

plasterboard, corner jointing tape bande renfort d'angle *f*

plasterboard, firecheck plaque de plâtre feu *f*

plasterboard, fireproofed plaque de plâtre ignifugée *f*

plasterboard, flooring plaque de plâtre de sol *f*

plasterboard, high density plaque de plâtre haute densité *f*

plasterboard, jointing tape bande à joint *f*

plasterboard with central insulating layer panneau de doublage plaque de plâtre *m*

plasticiser plastifiant *m*

plumbline fil à plomb maçon *m*

poleaxe merlin *m*

polyurethane polyuréthane *m*

porch porche *m*

powder poudre *f*

power tool accessories accessoires outillage électroportatif *m*

power tools, portable outillage électroportatif *m*

prefabrication préfabrication *f*

purlin panne *f*

purlin, eaves panne sablière *f*

purlin, ridge panne faîtière *f*

putty pâte *f*; mastic *m*

radiator reflector plaque isolante et réfléchissante *m*

rafter chevron *m*

rafter, hip arêtier *m*

refurbish remettre à neuf *v*

refuse déchet *m*

reinforcement armature *f*

reinforcement (partition framework) montant métallique *m*

render, to enduire *v*

rendering crépi *m*; crépissage *m*; enduit *m*

renovate, to rénover *v*; restaurer *v*

renovation rénovation *f*

repointing rejointoiement *m*

resin binder résine d'adjonction *f*

resin, colourless (to protect and reinforce concrete slab) traitement liquide incolore à base de résines *m*

resin, latex-based résine à base de latex *f*

restoration mortar kit for concrete mortier réparation kit *m*

resurface, to refaire la surface *v*

resurfacing ravalement *m*

ridge bar longeron de faîtage *m*

ridge, roof faîtage *m*

riser, staircase contremarche *f*

rockwool laine de roche *f*

rockwool flakes (in bulk) flocons de laine de roche en vrac *m*

rockwool panel panneau laine de roche *m*

rockwool panel, unsurfaced panneau laine de roche non revêtue *m*

rockwool triangle triangle de laine de roche *m*

roll rouleau *m*

roll, reflective roof insulation rouleau multi-réflecteur *m*

roof toit *m*

roof, flat toit-terrasse *m*

roof, glass verrière *f*

roof tile tuile *f*

roof verge rive de toit *f*

room pièce *f*

roughcast, to crépir *v*;
hérissoner *v*

roughcasting crépissage *m*

router défonceuse *f*

RSJ (rolled steel joist) poutre
en fer *f*

rule (darby) règle de maçon *f*

rule, folding mesure pliante *f*

sand sable *m*

sand, bulk quantity sable en
vrac *m*

sand, concreting sable de
mélange béton *m*

sand, masonry sable à
maçonner *m*

sand, river sable de rivière *m*

sand, sharp sable liant *m*; ~
mordant *m*

sand, soft sable doux *m*

sand, silver sable argenté *m*

sandblaster sableuse *f*

sander ponceuse *f*

sander, belt ponceuse à bande *f*

sander, delta ponceuse delta *f*

sander, disc ponceuse
excentrique *f*

sander, orbital ponceuse
vibrantes *f*

sandstone grès *m*

saw scie *f*

saw blade lame de scie *f*

saw, chain tronçonneuse *f*

saw, circular scie circulaire *f*

saw, jig scie sauteuse *f*

saw, sabre scie sabre *f*

scaffold board planche
d'échafaudage *f*

scaffolding échafaudage *m*

screed chape *f*

**screwdriver (with or without
cord)** visseuse *f*

seal, to sceller *v*

sealant enduit étance *m*

semi-detached jumelé -e *adj*

serving hatch passé plat *m*

set accelerator accélérateur
rapid *m*

setting agent fixateur *m*

sewer, mains tout a l'égout *m*

**shingle, bituminous felt
roof** bardeau (*pl* -x) verrier
bitumen *m*

shingle, roof bardeau (*pl* -x) *m*

shovel pelle *f (see also: spade)*

shovel, round pelle ronde *f*

shovel, square pelle carrée *f*

shuttering release agent
décoffrage décoffre *m*

sieve tamis *m*

skip benne *f*

skirting board plinthe *f*

slab lifter pose-dalle *f*

slate, fibre cement roofing ardoise fibres-ciment *f*

slate fixing hook crochet ardoise *m*

slate, roofing ardoise *f*

sound insulating cork wall tile dalle liège mur spécial isolation phonique *f*

sound insulation, damp floors isolation phonique pour sol humide *f*

soundproof membrane (floors) isolation phonique sols *f*

soundproofing isolation acoustique *f*

spade bêche *f*; pelle *f (see also: shovel)*

spindle -s, banister fuseau (*pl* -x) *m*

spraying machine (Tyrolean) machine à crépir (tyrolienne) *f*

square, builder's équerre du maçon *f*

staircase escalier *m*

staircase, quarter turn at base escalier quart tournant bas *m*

staircase, quarter turn at centre escalier quart tournant milieu *m*

staircase, quarter turn at centre, with landing escalier quart tournant milieu avec palier *m*

staircase, quarter turn at top escalier quart tournant haut *m*

staircase, spiral escalier spirale *m*; ~ en colimaçon *m*; ~ tournant *m*; ~ à vis hélicoïdal carré *m*

staircase, straight escalier droit *m*

staircase, two quarter turns escalier deux quarts tournants *m*

stairwell cage escalier *f*

staple (hammer-in) crampillon *m*

staple gun agrafeuse *f*

steel acier *m*

stepladder escabeau *f*

stone pierre *f*

string, builder's cordeau de maçon *m*

string, open staircase crémaillère *f*

string, staircase limon *m*

string, wall staircase faux limon *m*

support prop étai *m*

taping knife couteau à joint pour plaques d'isolation *m*

tarpaulin bâche *f*

thatch chaume *m*

thermal/heat insulation isolation thermique *f*

thermal/sound insulating tile dalle isolante/phonique *f*

tile adhesive ciment colle *m*

tile, ceiling dalle de plafond *m*

tile, ceramic carreau de faïence *m*

tile, floor carreau *m*

tile, gutter tuile creuse *f*

tile, half-round tuile romaine *f*

tile, interlocking flat tuile plate à emboîtement *f*; ~ à emboîtement à pureau plat *f*

tile, interlocking roman (large mould, deep curve) tuile romaine grande moule fortement galbée *f*

tile, interlocking ribbed tuile à côtes *f*

tile, interlocking shallow curved tuile à onde douce *f*; **(large mould, shallow curve)** ~ à emboîtement grande moule faiblement galbée *f*; **(small**

mould, shallow curve) ~ à emboîtement petit moule faiblement galbée *f*

tile, plain tuile plate *f*

tile, ridge tuile faîtière *f*

tile, roofing tuile *f*

tile, terracotta carreau de terre cuite *m*

tile, to carreler *v*

tile, transparent tuile en verre transparente *f*

tile, ventilator tuile à douille *f*; ~ à chatière grillagée *f*

tile, verge tuile de rive *f*

tile, wall carreau *m*; plaquette *f*

tiling carrelage *m*

tiling batten, roof liteau couverture *m*

toolbox boîte à outils *f*; porte-outils *m*

transom traverse *f*

tread, staircase marche *f*

treatment for bases traitement sols *m*

treatment for bases, colourless waterproofing imprégnation incolore, pavés et dalles béton *f*

treatment for bases, resin (to protect and reinforce

concrete slab) liquide incolore à base de resins *m*

treatment for cellars traitement caves et sous-sols *m*

treatment for cellars, waterproofing revêtement d'imperméabilisation pour travaux de cuvelages *m*

trellis treillis *m*

trench tranchée *f*; fossé *m*

trench, to dig a fossoyer *v*

trestle tréteau *m*

trough, mixing auge *f*

trowel truelle *f*

trowel, bricklaying truelle à brique *f*; **(rounded tip)** ~ ronde *f*; **(pointed tip)** ~ italienne *f*

trowel, bucket (square-edged) truelle carrée *f*

trowel, cement platroir à enduire *m*

trowel, corner truelle d'angle *f*

trowel, finishing platroir à enduire *m*

trowel, flooring platroir à enduire *m*

trowel, gauging truelle langue de chat *f* (nearest equivalent)

trowel, plaster mixing gâche *f*

trowel, plasterer's platroir à enduire *m*

trowel, pointing (English: pointed tip; French: rounded tip) truelle langue de chat *f*

trowel, notched platroir à enduire denté *m*

truss, roof armature à toit *f*; ferme de charpente *f*

underfelt, roof écran de sous-toiture *m*

vacuum cleaner (water and dust) aspirateur eau et poussières *m*

ventilation grille cour anglaise *f*

vermiculite vermiculite *f*

vermiculite, bitumen-coated vermiculite enrobée de bitume *f*

vermiculite, granulated granulé isolant vermiculite *f*

wainscot, to lambrisser *v*

wainscoting lambris *m*; lambrissage *m*

wall mur *m*

wall chaser attachment rainureuse *f*

wall, load-bearing mur portant *m*

wall, partition cloison *f*
wall, party mur mitoyen *m*
wall, to murer *v*
warp, to se déformer *v*
warping déformation *f*
water supply, mains eau de la ville *f*
waterproof; watertight; impermeable étanche *adj*
waterproof, to étancher *v*
waterproofing étanchéité *f*; imperméabilisant -e *adj*
waterproofing, colourless for paving and conrete slabs traitement imprégnation incolore, pavés et dalles béton *m*
waterproofing treatment for cellars traitement revêtement d'imperméabilisation pour travaux de cuvelages *m*
waterspout (guttering) gargouille *f*
wedge, log-splitting coin *m*
wheelbarrow brouette *f*
whitewash badigeon *m (see also: lime paint)*
whitewash, to badigeonner *v*
window fenêtre *f*
window, bay/bow oriel *m*

window, casement fenêtre à battants *f*
window, dormer lucarne *f*
window frame dormant *m*
window, French porte-fenêtre *f*
window, roof fenêtre de toit *f*
window, sash fenêtre à guillotine *f*
window sill rebord de fenêtre *m*
workbench établi *m*
wrecking bar pince a décoffrer *f*

NOTES

CARPENTRY

CHARPENTERIE

adze herminette *f*

arch cintre *m*

ash frêne *f*

assemble, to assembler *v*

assembly; assembling assemblage *m*

auger (for making pilot holes) vrille *f*

axe hache *f*

band saw scie à ruban *f*

banister balustre *m*

banister rail main courante *f*

banisters rampe d'escalier *f*

batten, flooring planche *f (see also: plank; board)*

baulk poutre *f*

beading/casing baguette *f*

beam poutre *f*

beam, cross traverse *f*

beam, exposed poutre apparentre *f*

beam, large madrier *m*

beam, main poutre maîtresse *f*; poutre principale *f*

beam, small poutrelle *f*

bedane (chisel for woodturning) bédane de menuisier *m*

beech hêtre *m*

bevel biseau *(pl -x) m (see also: chamfer)*

bevel, adjustable/sliding/ combination fausse équerre *f*

bevel, to biseauter *v (see also: chamfer, to)*

bevelled edge chanfrein *m*

blade lame *f*

block bloc *m*

block, sandpaper cale *f*

blockboard latté *m*

board planche *f (see also: batten, flooring; plank)*

board/plank, loose planche mobile *f*

bolt boulon *m*

border frise *f*

bore calibre *m*

bore, to percer *v*

boxing; framework; shuttering coffrage *m*

brace vilebrequin *f*

brad clou à tête perdue *m*; ~ étêté *m*; ~ sans tête *m*

bradawl tarière à gouge *f*

brushed brossé -e *adj*

buckling; warping déformation *f*

butt about *m*

butt, to abouter *v*

butt joint joint bout à bout *m*

carpenter charpentier *m*

carpenter's bench établi de bois *m*

carpenter's hammer hachette de charpentier *f*

carpenter's pencil crayon charpente *m*

ceiling plafond *m*

ceiling rose rosace de plafond *f*

chainsaw tronçonneuse *f*

chamfer chanfrein *m*

chamfer, to chanfreiner *v*

chipboard panneau d'aggloméré *m*; ~ de particules *m*

chisel, bevel-edged ciseau de menuisier *m*; ~ sculpteur *m*

chisel, firmer ciseau de charpentier *m*

chisel, mortise bédane de menuisier *m*

chisel, parting (woodturning) ciseau à grain d'orge *m*

chisel, skew (woodturning) plane *m*

chisel, straight (woodturning) ciseau droit *m*

chisel, to ciseler *v*

chisel -s, wood ciseau (*pl* -x) à bois *m*

clamp serre-jointe *m*

clamp, bar serre-joint automatique *m*

clamp, F-style gripper serre-joint à pompe *m*; presse mâchoire *m*

clamp, G- presse de mécanicien *f*

clamp, handy pince de serrage *f*

clamp, ratchet pince étau à cliquet *f*

clamp, sash grand serre-joint *m*

clamp, speed serre-joint automatique *m*

clamp, spring pince à ressort *f*

cleave, to refendre *v*

cleaving refente *f*

cleft fente *f*; gerce *f*

clip for T&G panelling, metal crochet à lambris *m*; clip à frisette *m*

corrugated fastener clou ondulé *m*

cross-halving joint assemblage à demis-bois *m*

decay pourrissement *m*

decay, to pourrir *v*

decorative border frise décorative *f*

dimensions dimensions *f*

door porte *f*

door edging couvre-chant *m*; alaise rapportée *f*

door frame huisserie *f*

door knob bouton de porte *m*

dovetail joint assemblage queue d'aronde *m*

dowel cheville *f*; tourillon *m*

dowel pin repère de tourillon *m*

draw, to tracer *v*; dessiner *v*

drawknife plane *m*

drill perceuse *f*

drill bit foret *m* *(see also: drill bit, twist)*

drill bit, auger foret vrille *m*

drill bit, expansive foret expansive *m*

drill bit, flat/spade mèche plate *f*

drill bit, twist foret *m*

drill, hand chignole *f*

drill, to percer *v*

dry rot pourriture sèche *f*

eaves avant-toit *m*

elm orme *m*

façade/frontage pelmet façade cantonnière *f*

false tongue (joint) fausse languette *f*

fascia board planche de rive *f*

fence post piquet de clôture *m*

fencing palissade *f*

file lime *f*

finish; finishing finition *f*

finish off, to ragréer *v*; parfaire *v*

fir sapin *m*

flat pack en kit *m*

flitch of timber (slab, cut lengthways from a tree trunk) dosse *f*

frame cadre *m*

framework charpente *f*

frieze frise *f*

gable pignon *m*

gate porte *f*

gate(s), wooden portail en bois *m*

gauge, caliper (woodturning) compas d'épaisseur *m*

gauge, marking/mortise trusquin *m*; troussequin *m*

gimlet tarière *f*

glasspaper papier de verre *m*

glue, to coller *v*

gouge (woodturning) gouge *f*

gouge, bottle gouge bouteille *f*

gouge, bowl gouge à creuser *f*

gouge, conical gouge conique *f*

gouge, roughing-out gouge à dégrossir *f*

gouge, spindle gouge à profiler *f*

grain (of wood) fil de bois *m*

grind, to affûter *v*

grinder affûteuse *f*

grinding affûtage *m*

grooved rainé -e *adj*

grooved end/tip rainé -e en bout *adj*

groove, to rainer *v*

hacksaw scie à métaux *f*

half-timbered colombage *m*

halving joint assemblage à mi-bois *m*

hammer -s marteau (*pl* -x) *m*

hammer, carpenter's marteau à menuisier *m*

hammer, claw marteau arache-clou *m*; ~ de coffreur *m*

hammer, packer's marteau d'emballeur *m*

handsaw scie à main *f*

hardboard isorel *m*; fibres dures *fpl*

hardwood bois dur *m*

hinge charnière *f*; gond *m*

hinge, door paumelle *f*

interlocking; fitting emboîtement *m*

iroko iroko *m*

jigsaw scie sauteuse *f*

joist solive *f*

joist, small soliveau (*pl* -x) *m*

knife couteau *m*

knives coutellerie *f*

knot noeud *m*

lacquer, to laquer *v*

lacquered laqué -e *adj*

lath latte *f*

lathe tour à bois *m*

lathe bed banc *m*

lathe copy turning attachment copieur universel *m*

lathe faceplate plateau de tournage *m*

lathe headstock poupée fixe *f*

lathe motor block bloc-moteur *m*

lathe spindle broche *f*

lathe tailstock poupée mobile *f*

lathe tool rest éventail *m*

length longueur *f*

length of wood tasseau (*pl* -x) *m*

linseed oil huile de lin *f*

mahogany acajou *m*

mallet maillet *m*

mallet, cabinet maker's (round head) maillet d'ébéniste *m*

mallet, woodwork (square head) maillet de menuisier *m*

maritime pine pin maritime *m*

mark out, to jalonner *v*

matchboard planche bouvetée *f*

MDF (medium density fibreboard) MDF *m*

measure, to mesurer *v*

mitre box boîte à onglets *f*

mortise mortaise *f*

mortise and tenon joint assemblage à tenon et mortaise *m*

moulding moulure *f*

moulding, astragal astragale *m*

moulding, cornice corniche *f*

moulding, cover strip couvre-joint *m*

moulding, cover strip (for tiles) couvre-joint carrelage *m*

moulding, cover strip (for walls) couvre-joint cloison *m*

moulding, flat edge chant plat *m*

moulding, framing encadrement *m*

moulding, half-round moulure demi-rond *f*

moulding, picture frame cimaise *f*

moulding, quarter-round quart-de-rond *m* (*pl* quarts-de-rond)

moulding, right-angle baguette d'angle *f*

moulding, rounded lip (for stairs) nez de marche *m*

moulding, window frame chambranle *m*

nail clou *m*; pointe *f*

nail, brass-headed clou doré *m*

nail, clout clou à tête diamant *m*

nail, cut clou découpé *m*; ~ étampé *m*

nail, extra large head clout clou à tête plate, 'extra large' *m*

nail, flooring clou à bateaux *m*

nail, lost head clou sans tête *m* (*see also: brad*)

nail, masonry clou à beton *m*

nail, oval wire clou tête d'homme *m*

nail punch chasse-clou *m*

nail, round wire clou à tête plate *m*

nail, to clouer *v*

nail, twisted shank clou torsadé *m*

nail, wire clou de Paris *m*

niangon niangon *m*

notch entaille *f*

notch, to entailler *v*

notching entaillage *m*

oak chêne *m*

oil huile *f*

oil, to huiler *v*

panel -s panneau (*pl* -x) *m*

panelling lambris *m*

parquet flooring parquet *m*

parquet, glued parquet à coller *m*

pin cheville *f*

pin, dome-headed upholstery pointe décorative à tête bombée *f*

pine pin *m*; **(from Landes region of France)** pin des Landes *m*

pine, solid pin massif *m*

plane rabot *m*

plane, block rabot fonte *m*

plane, hand/jack rabot manuel *m*; ~ semelle metal *m*

plane, **moulding** rabot moulure *m*

plane, rebate rabot guillaume *m*

plane, smoothing rabot métallique *m*

plane, to raboter *v*

planer file (Surform) rabot Surform *m*

plank planche *f (see also: batten, flooring; board)*

plank, thin volige *f*

plank (10" x 2½") bastaing *m*

plywood contre-plaqué *m*; contre-collé -e *m*

polished ciré -e *adj*

poplar peuplier *m*

pre-glued pré-encollé -e *adj*

purlin panne *f*

rafter/chevron chevron *m*

raftering chevronnage *m*

ramin ramin *m*

rasp râpe *f*

rifler file rifloir *m*

roofing batten liteau *m*

rosewood palissandre *m*

rounded arrondi -e *adj*

rule règle *f*

rule, flexible steel réglet inox flexible *f*

rule, folding mètre pliant *m*

sand, to poncer *v*

sand down, to poncer *v*

sander ponceuse *f*

sander, belt ponceuse à bande *f*

sander, delta ponceuse delta *f*

sander, disc ponceuse excentrique *f*

sander, orbital ponceuse vibrantes *f*

sandpaper papier de verre *m*

sandpaper, to poncer *v*

saw scie *f*

saw, all-purpose (for man-made boards and natural timber) scie égoïne universelle *f*

saw, band scie à ruban *f*

saw, carpenter's scie de charpentier *f*

saw, coping/fret scie à chantonner *f*

saw, cross-cut (for cutting across the grain) scie égoïne pour coupe transversal *f*

saw, frame scie à monture de menuisier *f*

saw, gents/back scie à araser *f*

saw, hand scie égoïne grosse coupe *f*; **(for constructional timber such as rafters, formwork and planks)** ~ à denture américaine *f*; **(for mouldings, panelling)** ~ égoïne coupe fine *f*

saw, mitre scie à onglet *f*

saw, pad scie à guichet *f*

saw, panel (for man-made boards and natural timber) scie à panneaux *f*

saw, rip (for cutting along the grain) scie égoïne pour coupe longitudinal *f*

saw, tenon scie à dos *f*

saw, to scier *v*

saw, veneer scie à placage *f*

scraper racloir de finition *m*; **(woodturning)** ciseau à racler arrondis *m*

screw, to visser *v*

sharpened/square cut avivé -e *adj*

shelf étagère *f*; tablette *f*

shellac laque *f*

shellac, to laquer *v*

shooting board planche à dresser *f*

shutter volet *m*

skirting board plinthe *f*

skirting board, veneered plinthe plaquée *f*

slate peg pointe à ardoise *f*

smooth lisse *adj*

smooth, to lisser *v*

solid massif -ive *adj*

softwood bois tendre *m*

splinter éclat *m*

split, to refendre *v*

spokeshave rabot racloir acier *m*; vastringue *f*

sprig, glazing clou de vitrier *m*

spruce épicéa *m*

stained; tinted teinté -e *adj*

staple agrafe *f*

strip of wood lame *f*

structure/framework charpente *f*

Surform tool Surform; rabot Surform *m*

tack pointe *f*; petit clou *m*; clou de bouche *m*; clou de soufflet *m*

tack, upholstery semence de tapissier *f*

teak teck *m*

tenon tenon *m*

thickness épaisseur *f*

timber bois de charpente *m*

timber frame charpente en bois *f*

timberwork boisage *m*

tree arbre *m*

try square équerre *f*

varnish vernis *m*

varnish, clear vernis clair *m*

varnish, matt vernis mat *m*

varnish, satin vernis satiné *m*

varnish, to vernir *v*

varnishing vernissage *m*

veining, wood veinage de bois *m*

veneering placage *m*

vice étau *m*

wainscot, to lambrisser *v*; boiser *v*

wainscoting lambris *m*; lambrissage *m*

walnut noyer *m*

weatherboarding planches de recouvrement *f*

wedge cale *f*

wedge, to caler *v*

wenge wengé *m*

white fir (from the north of France) sapin blanc du nord *m*

width largeur *f*

wood bois *m*

wood grain fibre de bois *f*

wood, planed bois raboté *m*

wood, roofing bois de couverture *m*

woodfiller mastic pâte à bois *m*

woodscrew vis à bois *f*

woodscrew, chipboard vis à bois et aggloméré *f*

woodscrew, cross-headed (Phillips) vis empreinte cruciforme (Phillips) *f*

woodscrew, cross-headed (Posidriv) vis empreinte cruciforme (Posidriv) *f*

woodscrew, cross-headed (TORX) vis empreinte cruciforme (TORX) *f*

woodscrew, domed slot-headed vis ronde fendue *f*

woodscrew, non-removable vis spéciale indesserrable *f*

woodscrew, plasterboard vis plaque de platre *f*

woodscrew, slot-headed vis à tête fendue *f*

woodscrew, slot-headed countersunk vis plate, fraisée et fendue *f*

woodscrew, slot-headed round topped vis fraisée bombée *f*

wood, untreated bois brut *m*

woodwork boiserie *f*

woodworm ver du bois *m*

workbench-vice, portable établi-étau *m*; ~ pliante et réglable *m*

NOTES

DECORATING

DECORATION

abrasive mesh grille abrasive *f*
abrasive paper papier abrasif *m*
abrasive stone pierre abrasive *f*
acetone acétone *f*
awning/pergola, exterior store
de pergola *m*; housse store
extérieur *f*
awning with base support
store sur pied *m*
blind store *m*
blind cleaner, venetian
nettoyeur pour store
vénitien *m*
blind, conservatory store pour
véranda *m*
blind, roller store enrouleur *m*
blind, roman store bateau *m*
blind, venetian store
vénitien *m*; ~ à lamelles
orientales *m*
blind, vertical store à lamelles
verticales *m*
bristle (of brush) poil *m*
brush brosse *f*
brush, badger brosse en poils
de blaireau *f*
brush, cleaning/washing
brosse à lessiver *f*
brush, colourwashing pinceau
pour effet badigeon *m*

brush, dragging (paint effect)
pinceau de tirage *m*; brosse
pour effet moucheté *f*
brush, extra thick brosse plate
extra-épaisse *f*
brush, flat lacquer brosse plate
à lacquer *f*
brush, glaze pinceau à glacis *m*
brush/painting equipment
cleaner nettoyant outils
peinture *m*
brush, soft (paint effects)
brosse douce *f*
brush, stain/wood treatment
pinceau lasure, traitement des
bois *m*
brush, stencil pinceau *m*;
pochoir *m*
brush, stippling brosse à
pocher *f*
brush, synthetic soft (paint
effects) brosse douce
synthétique *f*
brush, to brosser *v*
brush, varnishing pinceau
spécial vernis *m*
bucket -s seau (*pl* -x) *m*
carpet; carpeting moquette *f*
carpet, Berber moquette
berbère *f*

carpet, cocoa fibre moquette fibres de coco *f*

carpet, looped moquette bouclée *f*

carpet, printed moquette imprimée *f*

carpet, raised pile moquette à relief *f*

carpet, rush rabane jonc de mer *f*

carpet, velvet pile moquette velours *f*

carpet, woven moquette tressée *f*

carpet, wool moquette laine *f*

ceiling rose rosace de plafond *f*

ceramic tile file râpe à céramique *f*

ceramic tile nibblers bec-de-perroquet *m*

ceramic tile saw scie à découper *f*

chamois leather peau de chamois *f*

chipped/flaking écaillé -e *adj*

cleat taquet *m*; arrêt de cordon *m*

clump of bristles (of a paintbrush) touffe *f*

coat (of paint etc.) couche *f*

coat, base première couche *f*

colour; shade coloris *m*

colour chart nuancier chromatique *m*

colouriser, pearl-coloured concentré de pigments à effet nacré et coloré *m*

colourwashing badigeon coloré à la chaux *m*

comb, corrugated card (for combed effect) peigne en carton nodule *m*

comb, rubber (for combed effect) peigne en caoutchouc *m*

combed (paint effect) peigné -e *adj*

cork liège *m*

crackle glaze glacis à craqueler *m*

curtain -s rideau (*pl* -x) *m*

cutter coupe *f*

cutting ruler/metal straightedge règle de coup *f*

curtain ceiling bracket support plafond *m*

curtain corner bracket collier d'angle *m*

curtain cord pull; acorn cache noeud *f*; gland noeud *m*

curtain, net voilage *m*

curtain pulley poulie *f*

curtain rail/rod barre à rideaux *f*; tringle chemin de fer *f*

curtain, ready-made rideau prêt à poser *m*

curtain ring -s anneau (pl -x) à rideaux *m*

curtain wall bracket support simple mural *m*; support monobloc *m*

decor/decoration décor *m*

decorative décoratif -ive *adj*

degreaser dégraissant *m*

diamond tile-cutting disc disque diamant carrelage *f*

dragging (paint effect) technique de tirage *f*

drying accelerator, paint- accélérateur de séchage *m*

dusting brush époussette *m*

eyelet œillet *m*

extension handle (for roller) ralonge télescopique *f*

faux finish (paint effect) faux-finis *f*

ferrule (of a paintbrush) virole

filler remplissage *m*

float (for pressing down tiles) batte *f*

floorcovering, vinyl (in rolls) revêtement de sol en rouleaux vinyle *m*

frame cadre *m*

frame clamp serre-joint à cadre *m*

frame clamp, corner (with tensioning cord) équerre de serrage et cordeau de tension *f*

frame, to encadre *v*

framing encadrement *m*

frotting (rubbed paint effect) frottage *m*

glass cutter coupe-verre *f*

glass fibre fibre de verre *m*

glass fibre, anti-crack fibre de verre anti-fissure *f*

glass fibre fabric toile de verre *f*

glass fibre, fine mesh fibre de verre mini-maille *f*

glass fibre, non-inflammable fibre de verre non-inflammable *f*

glass fibre, prepainted fibre de verre prépeinte *f*

glaze glacis *m*

glaze acrylic glacis acrylique *m*

glaze, oil glacis à l'huile *m*

glaze, semi-transparent finishing patine de finition *f*

glaze, wax glacis à la cire *m*

gloss glose *f*

gloss laqué -e *adj*

glue colle *f (see also: paste)*

glue, border/frieze colle pour frise *f*; ~ renforcée frise *f*

glue, cork colle murale liège *f*

glue gun pistolet à colle *m*

glue syringe seringue à colle *f*

glue, to coller *v*

glue, touch up (for wallpaper) colle pour raccord *f*; ~ renforcée raccord *f*

gluing encollage *m*

graining (paint effect) veinure *f*

grout enduit *m*

grout, to jointoyer *v*

handle (of paintbrush) manche *m*

hardener durcisseur *m*

hawk/flat trowel taloche *f*

hemstitched ajouré -e *adj*

hog's hair bristle (of paintbrush) soie de porc *f*

hot air gun pistolet décapeur à air chaud *m*

insulating cork underlay sous-couche liège isol *f*

joint mastic (in tube) mastique fixation cartouche *m*

knee pad, tiler's genouillère *f*

knife -ves couteau (*pl* -x) *m*

knife, adhesive comb couteau à colle *m*

knife, craft cutter *m*

knife, filling riflard *m*

knife, paint scraping couteau de peintre *m*

knife, rotating razor rasoir rotatif *m*

knife, scraping (for pointing insulation panels) couteau à joint pour plaques d'isolation *m*

knife, smoothing (for filler) couteau à enduire *m*

lacquer; gloss paint peinture laquée *f*

lay, to poser *v*

linen lin *m*

linseed oil huile de lin *f*

marbling (paint effect) effet marbrant *m*

marquetry; inlaid work; mosaic marqueterie *f*

masked wall mur masqué *m*

masking (paint effect) bandes de couleur *fpl*

masking tape ruban adhésif de masquage *m*

matt mat -e *adj*

metal rule règle à émarger *f*

metallic finish métallisé -e *adj*

mitre box (for cutting ceiling mouldings and cornices) boîte à coupe (moulures et corniches de plafond) *f*

mixer mélangeur *m*

moulding, decorative moulure decorative *f*

muslin etamine *f*

net; veil voile *m*

non-yellowing ne jaunit pas *expr*

paint peinture *f*

paint, acrylic peinture acrylique *f*

paint, anti-condensation peinture anti-condensation *f*

paint, bottle (for stencils) peinture en flacon *f*

paint, ceiling peinture pour plafond *f*

paint effects effets de peinture *mpl*

paint, emulsion peinture émulsion *f*

paint, fluorescent peinture fluo *f*

paint, gloss peinture brillante *f*

paint, interior wood peinture pour boiseries intérieures *f*

paint, masonry peinture façade *f*

paint, matt peinture mate *f*

paint mixer malaxeur de peinture *m*

paint, non-drip peinture antigoutte *f*

paint, odourless peinture inodore *f*

paint, oil-based peinture glycéro *f*

paint, one-coat peinture monocouche *f*

paint pad tampon à peindre *m*

paint palette palette à peindre *f*

paint roller -s rouleau (*pl* -x) à peindre *m*

paint, satin peinture satinée *f*

paint shield spatule à maroufler *f*

paint, spray peinture en aérosol *f*

paint spraygun pistolet à peinture *m*

paint thinner, cellulose diluant cellulosique *m*

paint thinner, synthetic diluant synthétique *m*

paint, to peindre *v*

paint, tube (for stencils) peinture en tube *f*

paint, two-coat peinture bicouche *f*

paint, wall peinture murale *f*

paint, white colourwash (for adding colorant) badigeon effet douceur blanc à colorer *m*

paintbrush brosse *f*; pinceau *(pl* -x*) f*

paintbrush, acrylic pinceau spécial acrylique *m*

paintbrush, ceiling brosse à plafond *f*

paintbrush, emulsion *(see: paintbrush, whitewash/emulsion/ paste)*

paintbrush, flat pinceau plat *m*

paintbrush (oil-based paint) pinceau spécial glycerol *m*

paintbrush, pointed (for delicate work) brosse à rechampir *f*

paintbrush, radiator (forward-angled) brosse radiateur coudée à plat *f*

paintbrush, radiator (side-angled) brosse radiateur coudée sur chant *f*

paintbrush, rectangular brosse rectangulaire *f*

paintbrush, round pinceau rond *m*

paintbrush, round-stock (rounded end to bristles) brosse de pouce *f*

paintbrush, small flat (for touching up and detailed/ artistic paintwork) brosse à tableaux plate *f*

paintbrush, small round (for touching up and detailed/ artistic paintwork) brosse à tableaux ronde *f*

paintbrush, sash (round-stock with rounded end to bristles) pinceau rond pouce *m*

paintbrush, touching up brosse à raccords *f*

paintbrush with tightly packed bristles brosse hermétique *f*

paintbrush, whitewash/ emulsion brosse à badigeon *f*

paintbrush, whitewash/ emulsion/paste (round-stock, large, squared end to bristles) brosse ronde *f*

painted peint -e *adj*

painting mitt, lambswool gant à peindre en peau de mouton *m*

palette knife sabre de tapissier *m*

paperhanging brush brosse de tapissier *f*

paste colle *f*; pâte *f* *(see also: glue)*

paste bucket seau à colle *m*

pasting brush brosse à encoller *f*

pasting table table à tapissier *f*

photograph frame cadre à poser *m*

picture frame saw scie d'encadreur *f*

plasterer's float/hawk taloche *f*

pliers pince *f*

pliers, ceramic tile pince coupe carrelage *f*

pliers, tiler's pince de carreleur *f*

putty mastic *m*

polish/shine remover décirant *f*

polish, to polir *v*

primer apprêt *m*; avant-peinture *m*; primaire *adj*

primer, metal antirouille primaire protecteur *m*

primer, stabilising durcisseur pour plâtre *m*

primer, wood sous-couche pour bois extérieurs *f*

rag chiffon *m*

rag rolling (paint effect) rouler au chiffon *v*

ragging (paint effect) essuyage *m*

redecorate, to réaménager *v*

restoration revalement *m*

restorer rénovateur *m*

retractable blade lame rétractable *f*

rod perche *f*

roller rouleau *m*; roulette *f*

roller, angled roulette spécial angle *f*

roller, coarse grain paint effect rouleau crépi gros grain *m*

roller, exterior rouleau façade *m*

roller, fine foam rouleau mousse fine *m*

roller, fine grain paint effect rouleau crépi grain fin *m*

roller, flocked foam rouleau en mousse floquée *m*

roller frame monture *f*

roller, lacquering/varnishing rouleau laqueur *m*

roller, honeycomb foam rouleau en mousse alvéolée *m*

roller, interior walls and ceiling rouleau murs et plafond *m*

roller, lined rouleau rayé *m*

roller, long fibre rouleau fibres longues *m*

roller, mini mini rouleau *m*

roller, mohair rouleau en mohair *m*

roller, natural lambswool rouleau mouton laine naturel *m*

roller, polyamide rouleau d'une polyamide tissée *m*

roller, radiator rouleau à radiateur *m*

roller, ribbed roulette angle nervurée *f*

roller, rubber rouleau en caoutchouc *m*

roller, short fibre rouleau fibres courts *m*

roller sleeve manchon *m*

roller, stain and fluid products rouleau pour lasure *m*

roller, synthetic foam rouleau de mousse synthétique expansée *m*

roller, textured paint roulette crépi grosse grain *f*

roller, texturing rouleau à effet *m*

roller tray bac spécial à réservoir *m*; égouttoir *m*

roller, varnish rouleau à vitrifier *m*

roller, wood rouleau pour les bois *m*

rubber-blade squeegee raclette à emmancher *f*; raclette à joint *f*

rubber gloves gants de caoutchouc *mpl*

rust inhibitor antirouille *m*

sand, to poncer *v*

sanded poncé -e *adj*

sanding block cale à poncer *f*

sandpaper papier de verre *m*

scissors ciseaux *mpl*

scissors, decorator's ciseaux de décoration *mpl*

scissors, heavy duty ciseaux gros travaux *mpl*

scissors, multi-use ciseaux multi-use/universel *mpl*

scraper/paint scraper racloir *m*

scratching blade grattoir à lame *m*

scumble (paint effect) frottis *m*

shave hook, triangular grattoir à fissures triangulaire *m*

softener assouplisseur *m*

solvent dissolvant *m*

spalter (brush for smoothing lacquer and varnish) spalter *m*

spatula spatule *f*

spatula, notched spatule
crantée *f*

sponge, natural éponge
naturelle *f*

sponge, synthetic éponge
synthétique *f*

sponging (paint effect)
tamponnage à l'éponge *m*

spray, to (liquid) pulvériser *v*;
(as a mist) vaporiser *v*

stain/tint lasure *f*

stain remover détachant *m*

stain, to tacher *v*

stained taché -e; teinté -e *adj*

stamp tampon *m*

**stamping and blocking
(paint effect)** tamponnage et
impression *m*

stencil pochoir *m*

stencilling copie au pochoir *m*;
flocage *m*

stippling (paint effect) pochage *m*

**stripper, biological stain
(removal of biological stains
from tiles)** décapant carrelage
spécial tâches organiques *m*

stripper, chemical paint
décolleuse de peint *f*

stripper, chemical wallpaper
décolleuse de papiers peints *f*

**stripper, grease stain
(removal of grease stains
from tiles)** décapant carrelage
spécial tâche de graisse *m*

**stripper, stain (removal of
cement stains from un-
glazed tiles)** décapant voile et
laitance ciment carrelage non
émaillé *m*

stripper, steam décolleuse *f*

**stucco (not generally
available in UK)** crépi *m*

stucco, to crépir *v*

**synthetic bristle (of
a paintbrush)** poil
synthétique *m*

thinner diluant *m*

turpentine térébenthine *f*

tile -s, carreau (*pl* -x) *m*

tile, carpet dalle moquette *f*

tile cement ciment joint *m*

tile, ceramic carreau
céramique *m*

tile cleaner nettoyant
carreaux *m*

tile, cork carreau liège *m*

tile joint sealant joint en pâte *m*

tile, large floor; paving stone
dalle *f*

tile, PVC carreau de sol en PVC *m*

tile, reconstituted stone
carreau pierre reconstituée *m*

tile sheen patine carreaux *f*

tile spacer croisillon *m*

tile transfer, self-adhesive
applique auto-collant *f*

tile, vinyl carreau vinyle *m*

tile waterproofer
imperméabilisant carreaux *adj*

tile wax/polish cire carrelage *f*

tile-cutter, electric coupe-
carrelage électrique *m*

tile-cutter, flat bed coupe-
carrelage manuel *m*

tile-cutters coupe-carrelage *m*

tiling carrelage *m*

**tray, ready-pasted wallpaper
soaking** encolleuse *m*

undercoat sous-couche *f*

**underlay, insulating cork
(fitted carpet)** sous-couche
liège isol moquette *f*

varnish vernis *m*

varnished verni -e *adj*

varnish, clear vernis clair *m*

varnish, coloured vernis
coloré *m*

varnish, gloss vernis brillant *m*

varnish, matt vernis mat *m*

varnish, satin vernis satiné *m*

varnish, yacht vernis marin *m*

wall cladding plaquette de
parement *f*

wallpaper papier peint *m*

wallpaper, (for painting)
papier peint à peindre *m*

wallpaper cutter, electric
découper électrique de papier
peint *m*

**wallpaper, dappled effect (for
painting)** papier peint effet
pommelé *m*

wallpaper, embossed papier
peint gaufré *m*

wallpaper, expanded vinyl
papier peint vinyle expansé *m*

wallpaper, mural papier peint
mur d'image *m*

wallpaper seam roller roulette
colleur ébonite *f*

wallpaper steam stripper
décolleuse à vapeur *m*

wallpaper, textile effect papier
peint motif textile *m*

wallpaper, to tapisser *v*

wallpaper trimming wheel
roulette d'arasement *f*; lame
d'arasement *f*

wallpaper, washable papier
peint lavable *m*

wallpaper, woodchip papier peint à peindre motif naturel (incrustation de copeaux de bois) *m*

wallpaper, woven effect papier peint effet tissé *m*

washable lessivable *adj*

washing liquid for paint lessive pour peinture *f*

white spirit white-spirit *m*

white spirit, odourless white-spirit inodore *m*

wire brush, hand-held brosse à la main métallique *f*

wire brush, rotary (for power drill) brosse à décaper *f*

wirecutters cisailles *fpl*

wire wool laine d'acier *f*

wood graining (paint effect) veinurage *m*

wood graining effect tool outil à veiner effet bois *m*

NOTES

ELECTRICITY

ELECTRICITE

accumulator accumalteur *m*

act as earth, to faire masse *v*

adapter adapteur *m*

adapter, European standard adapteur européen standard *m*

adapter, international adapteur internationaux *m*

adapter on extension lead prolongateur-adapteur *m*

aerial antenne *f*

alarm bell sonnerie d'alarme *f*

all poles omnipolaire *adj*

alternating alternatif -ive *adj*

alternating current (a.c.) courant alternatif *m*

alternator alternateur *m*

ammeter ampèremètre *m*

amp ampére *f*

amperage ampérage *m*

antenna antenne *f*

anti-interference antiparasite *adj*

anti-lightning protector parafoudre modulaire *m*; paratonnerre *m*

appliance appareil *m*

auxiliary auxiliaire *m*

bare nu -e *adj*

bare wire fil nu *m*

bathroom lighting appliques de salle de bain *fpl*

battery batterie *f*; accu *m*; pile *m*

battery charger chargeur *m*

battery, rechargeable accu rechargeable *m*

battery-operated à piles *adj*

battery torch lampe de poche *f*

bayonet bulb socket douille à baïonnette *f*

bipolar; two-pole; two-pin bipolaire *adj*

blow, to griller *v*

blow, to (a fuse) fondre un fusible *v*

boosting survoltage *m*

box coffret *m*; boîte *f*

branch (wire conductor) branchement *m*

branch box boîte de distribution *f*

break a circuit, to déclencher un circuit *v*

breakdown défaillance *f*

bulb ampoule *f*; lampe *f*

bulb holder douille *f*

burn out, to griller *v*

busbar (consumer unit) barrette *f*; peigne d'alimentation *m*

cable câble *m*

cable by the metre (for installation in conduit) câble rigide au mètre *m*

cable clip with screw fitting
serre-câble à cheville *m*
cable conduit baguette *f*
cable conduit, floor-fixed
baguette sol *f*
cable connector connecteur *m*
cable core fil conducteur *m (see
also: conductor)*
**cable core, blue PVC-
sheathed** câble rigide, bleu *m*
**cable core, green/yellow
striped PVC-sheathed** câble
rigide, vert/jaune *m*
cable core, red PVC-sheathed
câble rigide, rouge *m*
cable cutter coupe-câble *m*
cable detector détecteur de
câbles *m*
**cable, EDF-installed for
meter connection** câble
téléreport armé *m*
cable, electric câble électrique *m*
cable exit sortie câble *f*
cable, extension câble
prolongateur *m*
cable, hi-fi câble hi-fi *m*
cable, mains câble de
distribution *m*
cable, multiwire câble
multifilaire *m*

cable reel câble enrouler *m*
**cable, silicone-sheathed (for
use in hot atmospheres)**
câble silicone *m*
cable socket borne de câble *f*
cable, telephone câble
téléphone *m*
cable terminal/termination
embout de câble *m*
capacitor condensateur *m*
casing moulure *f*
category catégorie *f*
charge charge *f*
circuit circuit *m*
circuit breaker coupe-circuit
m; disjoncteur *m (see also:
residual current device)*
circuit breaker, fused coupe-
circuit à fusible *m*
circuit closer commutateur
conjoncteur *m*
circuit connection connecteur
de circuit *m*
circuit diagram montage
électrique *m*
circuit wiring câblage de
circuit *m*
class catégorie *f*
clip pince de fixation *f*
clip, crocodile pince crocodile *f*

clip, to clipser *v*

close, to fermer *v*

close a circuit, to fermer *v* un circuit

closed circuit circuit fermé *m*

colour couleur *f*

component élément *m*

conduction conduction *f*

conductor conducteur *m (see also: cable core)*

conductor, earth conducteur de protection (terre) *m*

conductor, live conducteur de phase *m*

conductor, neutral conducteur de neutre *m*

conduit conduit *m*

connect, to connecter *v*; accoupler *v*; coupler *v*

connect in parallel, to coupler en parallèle *v*

connect in series, to coupler en série *v*

connection branchement *m*; connexion *f*; couplage *m*

connection, series couplage en série *m*

connection box boîte de distribution *f*

connector connecteur *m*

connector block dés de raccordement (dominos) *m*

connector, flex or cable connecteur direct *m*

consumer unit tableau de répartition *m*

consumer unit casing tableau électrique, coffret vide *m*

consumer unit pre-fitted with MCBs and RCD tableau pré-équipé *m*

consumer unit terminal borne de raccordement *f*

consumption dépense *f*; consommation *f*

contact contact *m*

continuous continu -e *adj*

control device appareil de commande *m*

control switch interrupteur de contrôle *m*

convector convecteur *m*

cooker cuisinière *f*

copper cuivre *m*

cord cordon *m*

cordless sans fil *adj*

couple, to raccorder *v*

coupling accouplement *m*

crimp connector cosse *f*

current courant *m*

current, direct (d.c.) courant direct *m*

cut, power coupure *f*

cut, to couper *v*

cut off the power, to couper le courant *v*

cut off power from, to délester *v*

dead hors courant

dead wire fil hors courant *m*

detector, break-in (alarm system) détecteur d'ouverture ou de chocs *m*

detector, carbon monoxide détecteur de monoxide de carbone *m*

detector; detection device détecteur *m*

detector, electrical current cut détecteur de coupure de courant *m*

detector, flood détecteur d'inondation *m*

detector, frost détecteur de gel *m*

detector, movement (alarm system) détecteur de mouvement *m*

detector, smoke détecteur de fumée *m*

detector, specialist détecteur technique *m*

diagram schéma *m*

dimmer switch variateur interrupteur *m*

disconnect, to déconnecter *v*

disconnection coupure *f*

dishwasher lave-vaisselle *m*

divert, to dériver *v*

doorbell sonnerie *f*

dynamo dynamo *f*

earth terre *f*

earth cable, bare copper câble de mise à la terre, cuivre nu *m*; câblette de terre *m*

earth, to mettre à terre *v*

earthed au sol *adj*

earthing mise à la terre *f*

earthing spike piquet de terre *m*

electric; electrical électrique *adj*

electric shock choc électrique *m*

electrical conductor conducteur électrique *m*

electrical socket outlet prise électrique *f (see also: socket)*

electricity électricité *f*

electricity supply alimentation en électricité *f*

electrification électrification *f*

electromagnetic
électromagnétique *adj*

electrostatic électrostatique *adj*

element élément *m*

equipment appareillage *m*;
équipement *m*

extension lead cordon
prolongateur *m*

exterior lighting accessories
appareils éclairage extérieur
mpl

extension cable ralonge *f*

failure défaillance *f*

fault défaillance *f*; défaut *m*

filament fil *m*

fittings équipement *m*

flex câble souple *m*

**flex by the metre (for
installation in conduit)** câble
souple au mètre *m*

flex core, PVC-sheathed câble
unifilaire souple *m*

flex reel câble souple en bobine *m*

flex, twin-core sheathed hi-fi
câble haut parleur, translucide,
méplat *m*

flow of electricity écoulement
d'électricité *m*

fluorescent tube tube
fluorescent *m*

freezer alarm détecteur de
panne de congélateur *m*

**French electricity supply
company** EDF (Electricité de
France)

frequency fréquence *f*

fuse fusible *m*

fuse board tableau de fusibles *m*

fuse box boîte à fusibles *f*;
fusible tabatière *m*

fuse, burnt out fusible grillé *m*

fuse, cartridge fusible à
cartouche *m*

fuse, ceramic fusible
céramique *m*

fuse holder porte-fusible *m*

fuse holder (porcelain fuses)
coupe-circuit à broche *m*

fuse, intact fusible bon

fuse tester testeur de fusibles *m*

fuse wire fil de plomb *m*

**fuse wire holder, brass (old-
type; no UK equivalent)**
plaquette fusible à fil de laiton *f*

gauge appareil de mesure *m*

generator dynamo *f*; générateur *m*

grid réseau *m*; grille *f*

grill grille *f*

halogen spotlight spot
halogène *m*

handyman's knife couteau d'électricien *m* (nearest equivalent)
heater appareil de chauffage *m*
hertz hertz *m*
high voltage haute tension *f*
intensity intensité *f*
intercom interphone radio *m*
insulating isolant -e; isolateur *adj*
insulation isolation *f*; isolement *m*
insulator isolant *m*; isolateur *m*
interrupt, to interrompre *v*
join, to raccorder *v*
joining raccordement *m*
joule joule *m*
junction dérivation *f*
junction box boîte de dérivation *f*
junction box cover couvercle dérivation *m*
lamp lampe *f (see also: light bulb)*
lamp base socle *m*
lampholder douille *f*
lampholder (one retaining ring) douille simple bague *f*
lampholder (two retaining rings) douille double bague *f*
lampholder, brass douille laiton *f*

leakage écoulement *m*
light bulb ampoule *f (see also: lamp)*
light bulb, bayonet cap culot B *m*
light bulb, clear lampe standard claire *f*
light bulb, clear incandescent (bayonet cap) ampoule standard claire, culot B *f*
light bulb, clear incandescent (screw cap) ampoule standard claire, culot E *f*
light bulb, energy-saving ampoule économie d'énergie *f*
light bulb, extra-low voltage halogen lampe halogène TBTS (très basse tension) *f*
light bulb, halogen ampule halogène *f*
light bulb, incandescent ampoule incadescente *f*
light bulb, incandescent reflector ampoule incadescente réflecteur *f*
light bulb, pearl/opal lampe standard dépolie *f*
light bulb, pearl/opal reflector réflecteur dépolie *f*
light bulb, screw cap culot E *m*

light fitting point lumineux *m*

light switch interrupteur *m*

light up, to allumer *v*

lighting éclairage *f*

lighting, automatic éclairage automatique *f*

lighting system réseau d'éclairage *m*

lightning foudre *f*

lightning rod parafoudre *m*; paratonnerre *m*

lightning voltage surge protector protection anti-foudre *f*

link up, to brancher *v*

live actif -ive *adj*; phase *f*

low voltage basse tension *f*; bas voltage *m*

low voltage current courant basse tension *m*

main fuse fusible principal *m*

main switch board tableau de commande principal *m*

main switch, consumer unit interrupteur différentiel *m*

mains voltage tension du secteur *f*

maximum voltage tension maximale *f*

measure, to mesurer *v*

measurement mesure *f*

miniature circuit breaker (MCB) disjoncteur divisionnaire différentiel *m*

moulding, surface-mounted PVC (for passage of electric cables) moulure *f*

mounting box boîte *f*

mounting box, ceiling boîte plafond *f*

mounting box, door/window frame boîte avec patte de chambranle *f*

mounting box, double or triple (switches and sockets) boîte, deux ou trois postes (interrupteurs et prises) *f*

mounting box for partition wall boîte appliquée cloison sèche *f*

mounting box for plasterboard wall, round boîte ronde, plaque de plâtre à encastrer *f*

mounting box, hollow partition boîte à encastrer pour cloison creuse *f*

mounting box, recessed boîte à encastrer *f*; boîte d'encastrement *f*

mounting box, recessed sealed boîte d'encastrement à sceller *f*

mounting box, solid wall boîte à encastrer pour mur plein *f*; ~ prise, mur plein *f*; ~ à encastrer pour prise *f*

mounting box, surface fixed boîte appliquée *f*

multiple socket adapter bloc multiprise *m*

multiple socket adapter, exterior bloc multiprise extérieur *m*

negative pole pôle négatif *m*

neutral neutre *adj*

nominal nominal -e (pl -x) *adj*

normal current courant de regime *m*

ohm ohm *m*

ohmmeter ohmmètre *m*

pilot light lampe témoin *f*

pin (of plug) broche *f*

pliers; pincers pince *f*

plug fiche *f*

plug in, to brancher *v*

plug, connector fiche de connexion *f*

plug, electric fiche électrique *f*

plug, female fiche femelle *f*

plug, male fiche mâle *f*

plug, male/female (live, earth) fiche mâle/femelle deux P+T (phase, terre) *f*

plug, rubber fiche caoutchouc *f*

plug, three-pin (live, neutral, earth) fiche trois P+N+T (phase, neutre, terre) *f*

plug, two-pin (live, earth) fiche deux P+T (phase, terre) *f*

plug, two-pole male/female fiche mâle/femelle deux pôles *f*

polarity polarité *f*

pole pôle *m*

pole, minus pôle moins *m*

pole, plus pôle plus *m*

pole, positive pôle positif *m*

power courant *m*; puissance *f*

power cut coupure *f*

power point prise de courant *f*

power supply alimentation de secteur *f*

principal consumer terminal borne d'arrivée *f*

protection protection *f*

protection sheathing gaine de protection *f*

pull-cord for installing cables in sheathing tire-fils *f*

push button bouton poussoir *m*

push switch poussoir à voyant *m*

put, to mettre *v*

put in place, to poser *v*

put power back on again, to rétablir *v* le courant

re-establish rétablir *v*

relay relais *m*

remote control switches and sockets interrupteurs et prises à distance *m*

removable amovible *adj*

residual current device (RCD) disjoncteur différentiel *m (see also: circuit breaker)*

resistance résistance *f*

screwdriver tournevis *m*

screwdriver, electrician's tournevis d'électricien *m*

screwdriver, Phillips tournevis pour vis Phillips *m*

screwdriver, tester tournevis testeur *m*

sealant enduit étanche *m*

sheathing, corrugated flexible cable gaine *f*

sheathing, plastic rigid gaine plastique rigide *f*

sheathing with pre-installed cable cores gaine préfilée *f*

sheathing with pre-installed circuit cable gaine précâblée *f*

short circuit court-circuit *m*

short circuit, to court-circuiter *v*

single-pole unipolaire *adj*

single wire unifilaire *adj*

socket prise *f (see also: electrical socket outlet)*

socket, double two-pole prise double deux pôles *f*

socket, recessed skirting board prise à encastrer plinthe *f*

socket, screw bulb douille à vis *f*

socket, surface-mounted prise en appliqué *f*

socket, telephone prise téléphone *f*

socket, telephone/computer prise téléphone/informatique *f*

socket, television/stereo/satellite prise TV/FM/SAT *f*

socket, three-hole plus earth prise trois P+T *f*

socket, two-hole plus earth prise deux P+T *f*

socket, two-hole with earth pin prise de terre *f*

socket, wall prise murale *f*

solar panel absorbeur *m*

source source *f*

spotlight projecteur *m*

spotlight, halogen (on telescopic tripod) projecteur halogène sur trépied télescopique *m*

spotlight, portable projecteur portable *m*

standard lamp lampadaire *m*

standard specification norme *f*

supply alimentation *f*

supply, to alimenter *v*

switch interrupteur *m*; bouton *m*

switch, foot-operated interrupteur à pied *m*

switch off, to couper *v*

switch on, to (light) allumer *v*

switch on, to (appliance) démarrer *v*; enclencher *v*

switch, programmable prise programmable *f*

switch, programmable digital prise digitale *f*

switch, programmable mechanical programmateur mécanique *f*

switch, trip disjoncteur *m*

switch, two-pole interrupteur bipolaire *m*

switch, surface-mounted interrupterur combiné pac saillie *m*

switchboard tableau de commutateurs *m*

system réseau *m*

terminal borne *f*

thermostat thermostat *m*

thread fil *m*

thread, to enfiler *v*

time clock, 24-hour horloge de programmation journalier *f*

time clock, 7-day horloge de programmation hebdomadaire *f*

timeswitch minuterie *f*

trailing socket bloc ménager *m*

transformer transformateur *m*

trip déclencheur *m*

trip, to déclencher *v*

triple pole; tripolar tripolaire *adj*

triple socket adapter triplite *m*

ultra-low voltage accessories appareils très basse tension *m*

unit élément *m*

volt volt *m*

voltage voltage *m*; tension *f*

voltmeter voltmètre *m*

wall-plug cheville *f*

washing machine lave-linge *m*

waterproof étanche *adj*

watertight étanche *adj*

watt watt *m*

wattage puissance *f*

wattmeter wattmètre *m*

wire fil *m*

wire, live fil de phase *m*

wire, neutral fil neutre *m*

wirecutters pince coupante *f*

wirestrippers, adjustable pince
  à dénuder réglable *f*

wirestrippers, multiple jaw
  pince à dénuder automatique *f*

wirestrippers, side-cutting
  pince à dénuder à becs *f*

wiring câblage *m*

work light baladeuse *f*

NOTES

FINANCIAL

FINANCIER

BANKING
TAX
INSURANCE

account compte *m*

automated teller machine (ATM) guichet automatique *m*

balance of account solde *f*

bank banque *f*

bank account compte bancaire *m*

bank charge agio *m*

bank counter guichet *m*

bank identity record relevé d'identité bancaire (RIB) *m*

bank transfer virement *m*

bank statement relevé de compte; extrait *m*

banker's draft chèque de banque *m*

banking bancaire *adj*

bounce a cheque, to rejeter un chèque *v*

bounced cheque chèque sans provision *m*

branch code code guichet *m*

bridging loan; finance crédit relais *m*

cash withdrawal retrait d'espèces *m*

cheque chèque *m*

cheque book chéquier *m*

coins; change monnaie *f*

current account compte courant; ~ de dépôts *m*

debit débit *m*

deposit dépôt *m*

deposit account compte à terme *m*

direct debit prélèvement *m*

endorse, to (the back of a cheque) endosser *v*

exchange rate taux de change *m*

habitation tax taxe habitation *f*

insurance assurance *f*

insure, to faire assurer *v*

insured assuré -e *adj*

insured party assuré -e *mf*

insurer assureur *m*

joint current account compte de dépôt joint *m*

life insurance assurance-vie *f*

mortgage crédit hypothécaire *m*

mutual insurance company mutuelle *f*

overdraft découvert *m*

overdrawn account compte débiteur *m*

personal loan prêt personnel *m*

PIN number code confidentiel *m*

previous balance ancien solde *f*

property tax taxe foncière *f*

public health insurance sécurité sociale *f*

receipt reçu *m*

remittance remise *f*

savings account compte
d'épargne *m*

supplementary insurance
assurance supplémentaire *f*

**take out an insurance policy,
to** contracter une assurance *v*

**take out insurance for
oneself, to** s'assurer *v*

tax taxe *f*; impôt *m*

withdrawal of money retrait
d'argent *m*

NOTES

IRONMONGERY

QUINCAILLERIE

ADHESIVES
WEATHERPROOFING
WALLPLUGS & FIXINGS
SECURITY

access control, magnetic card (security) contrôle d'accès carte magnétique *m*

adhesive adhésif *m (see also: glue)*

adhesive, acrylic underlay colle acrylique pour sous-couche *f*

adhesive, all-purpose easy fixing colle fix facile tous supports *f*

adhesive, ceiling rose and cornice colle pour rosaces et corniches *f*

adhesive, ceiling rose and moulding colle pour rosaces et moulures vinyles et expansées *f*

adhesive, ceiling tile colle pour dalles de plafond *f*

adhesive, ceramic tile colle carrelage pâte *f*

adhesive, cold process (for bitumen) colle à froid de rêvetement bitume *f*

adhesive, cork (floor and wall) colle pour liège sol et mur *f*

adhesive, cork wall tile colle murale liège *f*

adhesive, decorative frieze colle pour frises décoratives *f*

adhesive, epoxy resin colle résine époxydique *f*

adhesive, expanded polystyrene panel colle isolants mince polystyrène expansé *f*

adhesive, extruded polystyrene panel colle isolants mince polystyrène extrudé *f*

adhesive, fibreglass and textile wallcovering colle fibres de verre et revêtements textiles muraux *f*

adhesive, fibreglass fabric colle pour toile de verre *f*

adhesive foam pad fixer mousse double face *m*

adhesive, gap-filling colle de blocage *f*

adhesive, insulating roll colle pour rouleaux isolants *f*

adhesive, interior wall colle murale universelle *f*

adhesive, laminate and floating floor colle pour stratifié et flottant *f*

adhesive, latex textile colle latex naturel pour tissu *f*

adhesive, leather and rubber colle pour cuir et caoutchouc *f*

adhesive, mirror colle pour miroirs *f*

adhesive mortar (for plasterboard) mortier adhésif (pour plaque de plâtre et doublage) *m*

adhesive, multi-purpose flooring colle sol polyvalente *f*

adhesive, neoprene pipe lagging colle néoprène pour manchon d'isolation *f*

adhesive, parquet fooring colle spécial parquet *f*

adhesive paste colle en pâte *f*

adhesive, plastic colle plastique *f*

adhesive, plastic flooring and carpet colle sols plastiques et moquettes *f*

adhesive, polystyrene soundproofing colle polystyrène phonicolle *f*

adhesive, PVC joint and guttering colle pour PVC raccords et gouttières rigide *f*

adhesive, rapid-setting wood colle bois prise rapide *f*

adhesive, reinforced frieze colle renforcée frises *f*

adhesive, reinforced textile wallcoverings and fibre glass fabric colle renforcée revêtements textiles muraux et toiles de verre *f*

adhesive, repositionable colle universelle repositionnable *f*

adhesive, rigid plastic colle pour plastique rigide *f*

adhesive, silicone colle silicone *f*

adhesive, solvent-free colle sans solvant *f*

adhesive tape ruban adhésif *m*

adhesive tape, all-purpose soft PVC adhésif PVC souple multi-usages *m*

adhesive tape, aluminium adhésif pour aluminium *m*

adhesive tape, anti-slip adhésif anti-dérapant *m*

adhesive tape, canvas-backed adhésif toile *m*

adhesive tape, double-sided adhésif double face *m*

adhesive tape, double-sided exterior grade adhésif double face extérieur *m*

adhesive tape, extra strong double-sided adhésif double face extra fort *m*

adhesive tape, leak repair
adhésif anti-fuites *m*

**adhesive tape, mirror fixing
double-sided** adhésif double
face miroirs *m*

**adhesive tape, plasterboard
jointing** adhésif raccord
plaques de plâtre *m*

**adhesive tape, protective
(corners and curves)** adhésif de
masquage courbe protection *m*

**adhesive tape, protective
(straight edges)** adhésif
masquage droit protection *m*

**adhesive tape, PVC (mineral
fibre and glass fibre
insulation)** adhésif PVC
rigide pour laine de roche laine
de verre *m*

**adhesive tape, reparing and
reinforcing** adhésif réparer/
renforcer *m*

adhesive tape, soft PVC
adhésif PVC souple *m*

adhesive tape, translucent
adhésif translucide *m*

adhesive, textile wallcovering
colle pour textiles muraux *f*

adhesive, thick wallpaper
colle pour papiers peints épais *f*

adhesive, transparent drying
colle transparente après
séchage *f*

**adhesive, vinyl (interior
wood)** colle vinylique pour
bois intérieur *f*

**adhesive, vinyl (exterior
wood)** colle vinylique pour
bois extérieur *f*

**adhesive, vinyl (paper and
cardboard)** colle vinylique
pour papier et carton *f*

adhesive, wallboard colle pour
plaquettes et parement *f*

**air pressure sensor dectector
(security)** détecteur
perivolumetrique alarme
électrique *m*

alarm alarme *f*

**alarm, appliance (radio
transmitted)** détecteur de
coupure secteur *m*

alarm, autonomous alarme
autonome *f*

alarm, door alarme pour porte *f*

alarm, entry avertisseur
d'entrée *m*

**alarm, infrared motion
detector** alarme autonome
infrarouge *f*

alarm kit, compact kit alarme sans fil compact *m*

alarm, magnetic door alarme à déclenchement magnétique *f*

alarm system kit, apartment kit alarme sans fil appartement *m*

alarm, window alarme de fenêtre *f*

alloy alliage *f*

aluminium case valise alu *f*

anchor fixing cheville métallique *f*

anchor fixing, nylon cheville nylon à expansion *f*

anchor fixing with screw cheville métallique et vis *f*

anchor fixing with screw, nylon cheville nylon à expansion avec vis *f*

anchor fixing without screw, nylon cheville nylon à expansion sans vis *f*

angle clamp presse d'angle *f*

angle plate équerre d'angle *f*

antenna antenne *f*

anti-bolt cutter security bar barre antipanique coupe feu *f*

anti-tamper case (with keyswitch and key) boîtier autoprotège (avec serrure à clef impulsion) *m*

axle arbre *m*

battery (toys, watches etc.) batterie *f*; pile *f*

bearing coquille *f*

bit fer *m*

bolt pêne *m* (lock); verrou *m* (lock); boulon *m* (hardware)

bolt, anchor boulon d'ancrage *m*

bolt, assembling boulon d'assemblage *m*

bolt, barrel verrou à coquille *m*

bolt, cotter boulon à clavette *m*

bolt, countersunk-head boulon à tête fraisée *m*

bolt, door targette *f*

bolt, foundation boulon de fondation *m*

bolt, French window locking espagnolette crémone *f*

bolt, hook boulon à croc *m*

bolt, locking verrou de fermeture *m*

bolt, retaining boulon de retenue *m*

bolt, round-head boulon à tête ronde *m*

bolt, screw boulon à ecrou *m*

bolt, slide verrou à plaquer *m*

bolt, spring verrou à ressort *m*

bolt, square-head boulon à tête carrée *m*

bracket, metal console métallique *f*

bracket, wall console murale *f*

castor roulette *f*

cavity fixing, steel spring toggle cheville en acier à ressort *f*; **(with hook)** ~ avec crochet *f*; **(with eye)** ~ avec piton *f*; **(with screw)** ~ avec vis *f*

chest malle *f*

clamp, joiner's serre-joint *m*

code keypad (alarm) clavier de codage *m*

collar collet *m*

combination lock cadenas à combinaisons *m*

combination lock, electronic serrure électronique à contrôle accès *f*

combination lock, programmable cadenas à combination programmable *m*

compartment compartiment *m*

control switch interrupteur *m*

corner coin *m*

corner plate équerre d'angle *f*

cover plate plaque de protection *f*

deadbolt pêne dormant *m*

deadlock, mortice serrure encastrer à clé *f*

detection cell, infrared cellule de détection infrarouge *f*

detector, floor contact détecteur contact de sol *m*

detector, gas détecteur de gaz *m*

detector, glass break détecteur de bris de glace *m*

detector, movement détecteur de movement *m*

detector, photoelectric détecteur à cellule photoélectrique *m*

detector, shock (windows) détecteur de choc *m* (fenêtre)

detector, smoke détecteur de fumée *m*

doorbell bouton de sonnette *m*

doorbell button bouton poussoir d'appel *m*

door chain chaînette de sécurité *f*

door chime carillon *m*

door chime, portable wireless carillon sans fil portée *m*

door closer ferme-porte *m*

door closer, automatic ferme-porte automatique *f*

door closer, spring ferme-porte à ressort *f*

door contact contacteur de porte *m*

door contact, wired alarm system contact de porte supplémentaire pour alarme *m*

door guard/chain entrebâilleur *m*

door knob bouton de tirage *m*

door knocker marteau (*pl.* -x) de porte *m*

door lock, base serrure bas de porte *f*

door lock, exterior déverrouillage externe *m*

door lock, top serrure haut de porte *f*

door roll draught excluder dessous de porte *m*

doorstop butée de porte *f*

door strip, adhesive (rain deflector/draught excluder/ sound insulator) bas de porte eau/air/bruit adhésif *m*

door strip, bronze heavy-duty brush bas de porte bronze (brosse dure) *m*

door strip, brush bas de porte brosse *m*

door strip, brush (garage) bas de porte garage brosse *m*

door strip, flapped bas de porte à bavette *m*

door strip, lipped bas de porte à lèvres *m*

door strip, pivoting bas de porte pivotant *m*

door strip, silver heavy-duty brush bas de porte argent (brosse dure) *m*

door strip, soft brush bas de porte brosse souple *m*

door viewer judas *m*

double-sided tape, multi-purpose adhésif double face multi-usages *m*

draught strip, foam bourrelet *m*

draughtproofing calfeutrage *m*

drawer runner coulisse de tiroir *f*

drawing pin punaise *f*

dummy siren/light sirène/flash factice *f*

entryphone/intercom portier électronique *m*

epoxy adhesive steel syringe colle epoxy acier seringue *f*

escutcheon plate rosace *f*; ~ à clé *f*

escutcheon with keyhole
rosace avec entrée de clé *f*

**excluder strip (draught/rain/
sound)** bas de porte *m*

eyelet œillet *m*

fire cement colle pour joint de
foyers et inserts *f*

fitments équipement *m*

fixing clip attache de fixation *f*

**flap seal, large thermoplastic
(garage)** bas de porte de
garage grande bavette *m*

**flap seal, small thermoplastic
(garage)** bas de porte garage
petite bavette *m*

garage door automation kit
kit motorisation porte garage *m*

gate automation motorisation
de portail *f*

gate security bar verrou de
sécurité portail *m*

gate spring, self-closing
ferme-porte à ressort spirale *f*

glue colle *f (see also: adhesive)*

**glue, cyanoacrylate
(porcelain and
earthenware)** colle
cyanoacrylate porcelaine et
faïence *f*

glue, epoxy colle époxy *f*

glue, epoxy glass colle époxy pour
verre *f*

glue, epoxy metal colle époxy
pour métal *f*

**glue, epoxy plastics and
vinyl** joint pour revêtements
plastiques et vinyliques *m*

glue, epoxy universal colle
époxy universelle *f*

glue, epoxy wood colle époxy
pour bois *f*

glue, fabric colle pour tissu *f*

glue gun pistolet à colle *m*

glue gun, cordless pistolet à
colle sans fil *m*

**glue gun, high temperature
hot melt** pistolet à colle haute
température *m*

glue gun, low melt pistolet à
colle à basse température *m*

glue gun nozzle buse pour
pistolet à colle *f*

**glue gun, variable
temperature** pistolet à
colle avec sélecteur de
température *m*

glue, jigsaw puzzle colle
acrylique pour puzzle *f*

glue, model colle pour
maquette *f*

glue, neoprene fixing fixation néoprène cartouche *f*

glue, neoprene liquid colle néoprène liquide *f*

glue, polymer colle polymère universelle *f*

glue, polystyrene colle polystyrène *f*

glue, polyurethane wood colle à bois polyuréthane *f*

glue, PVC colle PVC *f*

glue, repositionable stencil colle repositionnable spécial pochoir *f*

glue stick bâton de colle *m*; ~ colle *m*

glue stick, all-purpose bâton de colle multi-usage *m*

glue stick, bathroom/cables/ porous materials bâton colle pour sanitaire/câbles/matériaux poreux *m*

glue stick, heat sensitive materials bâton de colle pour matériaux sensibles à la chaleur *m*

glue stick, joints and earthenware bâton de colle pour joints et faïence *m*

glue stick, leather bâton colle pour cuir *m*

glue stick, metal bâton colle pour métaux *m*

glue stick, PVC and cables bâton de colle pour PVC et câbles *m*

glue stick, textiles and cork bâton colle pour textile et liège *m*

glue stick, wood and derivatives bâton de colle pour bois et dérivés *m*

glue syringe seringue à colle *f*

glue, textile colle textile *f*

glue, vinyl colle vinylique *f*

handle, door poignée de porte *f*

handle, furniture poignée d'ameublement *f*

handset/receiver combine audio supplémentaire *m*

hasp and staple porte-cadenas *m*

hacksaw blade lame de scie à métaux *f*

high security bolt verrou haute sécurité *m*

hinge ferrure *f*

hinge bolt, reinforcing security paire de renfort paumelles *m*

hinge, split paumelle *f*

hinge, spring charnière à ressort *f*

hook agrafe *f*

hook and hinge gond *m* et penture *f*

hook, picture crochet à tableau *m*

hook, wall gâche *f*

hooks and eyes pitonnerie *f*

infrared sensor interrupteur crépusculaire *m*

integrated siren centrale-sirène intégrée *f*

iron fer *m*

iron fittings ferrure *f*

key clé *f*

key cabinet coffre à clés *m*; armoire à clé *f*

keyhole trou de cylinder *m*

keyswitch commande à clé *f*

knob bouton *m*

knob, milled bouton moleté *m*

knuckle, hinge charnon *m*

L-iron fer d'angle *m*

latch loquet *m*

letter box boîte aux lettres *f*

lock serrure *f*

lock, combination cadenas a combinaisons *m*

lock, cylinder barillet *m*

lock cylinder cylindre de serrure *m*

lock, double input verrou double entrée *m*

lock, four tumbler serrure quatre gorges *f*

lock, horizontal surface-mounted serrure à appliquer horizontale *f*

lock, latch serrure à ressort *f*

lock, mortice serrure encastrée *f*

lock, multipoint serrure multipoints *f*

lock reinforcement bar bride de renfort *f*

lock, spring serrure à ressort *f*

lock, surface-mounted serrure en applique *f*

lock, vertical surface-mounted serrure à appliquer verticale *f*

lock, tubular serrure tubulaire *f*

locking bar (top and bottom of door) paire de verrous *m*

locking bar (wooden shutters) poignée verrou de sécurité volet bois *f*

locking bar, multipoint serrure à bandeau *f*

locking bar, three-point serrure trois points *f*

locking device condamnation *f*

masking tape adhésif protection toutes peintures bois/murs/peints *m*; ~ protection toutes peintures vitres/carrelages *m*

mastic adhesive mastic colle *m*

mastic adhesive, auto/marine mastic colle auto/marine *m*

mastic adhesive, glass and window mastic colle verre-vitrage cartouche *m*

metal case, articulated trays caisse métallique à plateau *f*

moldable adhesive pâte à coller *f*

motion detector, pet immune détecteur special animaux domestiques *m*

nailless/screwless adhesive colle ni-clou ni-vis *f*; **(cartridge)** ~ extrême cartouche *f*; **(tube)** ~ tube *f*

night latch (with moving bar) verrou sûreté à bouton *m*

nut écrou *m*

nut, blind écrou borgne *m*

nut, hexagonal écrou à six pans *m*

nut, locking écrou de blocage *m*

nut, square écrou carré *m*

nut, standard écrou ordinaire *m*

nut, wing écrou à oreilles *m*

nuts and bolts boulonnerie *f*

packaging tape adhésif emballage *m*

padlock cadenas à clef *m*

padlock, closed shackle cadenas anse protégée *m*

padlock, high security brass cadenas laiton haute sécurité *m*

padlock, laminated cadenas laminé *m*

padlock, long shackle cadenas anse haute *m*

padlock, solid brass cadenas laiton massif *m*

panic button, wireless bouton panique sans fil *m*

paste, non-woven wallcovering colle papiers intissés *f*

paste, universal wallpaper colle papier peints universelle *f*

paste, vinyl wallpaper colle papier peints vinyls *f*

paste, wallpaper colle papier peints *f*

photocell cellule photoélectrique *f*

pin cheville *f*

pin, uphostery clou tapissier *m*

pin, veneer pointe à placage *m*

pivot pivot *m*

plug and insertion tool set ensemble cheville et pince *m*

plug, expanding brass (suspended ceiling) cheville en laiton fendue pour plafond suspendu *f*

plug, expanding nylon cheville nylon fendue *f*

plug, nylon frame fixing (doors and windows) cheville nylon fendue pour encadrement de portes et fenêtres *f*

plug, hammer-in cheville à frapper *f*

plug, hammer-in nylon cheville nylon à clouer *f*

plug, mini hammer-in cheville mini *f*

plug, nylon cheville nylon *f*

plug, nylon (breezeblocks) cheville nylon spécial béton cellulaire *f*

plug, nylon block fixing cheville nylon à visser *f*

plug, plasterboard (hollow wall anchor) cheville plaque de plâtre *f*

plug, security grille cheville anti-effraction indémontable *f*

plug, steel cheville en acier *f*

portable tool bag baladeur à outils *m*

radio alarm transmitter, armoured transmetteur téléphonique blindé *m*

reinforcing plate plaque de renfort *f*

remote control télécommande *f*

restrictor, shutter entrebâilleur de volet *m*

restrictor, window entrebâilleur de fenêtre *m*

rim lock, keylock and turn button verrou clé et bouton *m*

rim lock, moving bar and turn button verrou automatique *m*

rim lock, multipoint serrure trois points horizontale à tirage *f*

ring bague *f*

ring, split anneau brisé *m*

rivet rivet *m*

rivet, round-headed rivet à tête ronde *m*

roller cabinet servante *f*

roller cabinet, builder's baraque de chantier *f*

runner rouleau *m*

S-plate ancre en forme d'un S *m*

safe coffre-fort *m*

safe, wall coffre-fort à encastrer *m*

security sécurité *f*

security bar barre de sécurité *f*

security bar (louvre shutter) barre de sécurité pour persienne *f*

security bar (shutter) barre de sécurité pour volet *f*

security bolt (roller shutter) verrou antipince-doigts pour volet roulant *m* **security grille** grille de défense *f*

security light, electric lampe électrique éclairage *f*

security light, electric halogen halogène électrique radar *f*

security light, infrared detector lampe détecteur infrarouge *f*

security lighting éclairage de sécurité *m*

self-adhesive pads pastilles adhésives *fpl*

self-drilling fixing cheville autoforeuse *f*

self-drilling fixing (frames and plasterboard) cheville autoforeuse vix cadre *f*

self-drilling fixings, case of mallette de chevilles autoforeuses *f*

self-drilling plasterboard fixing cheville autoforeuse à bascule *f*

self-screwing steel fixing cheville autoforeuse en acier à visser *f*

set square équerre *f*

sheet iron cover plaque en tôle *f*

shutter automation motorisation de volet *f*

shutter hinge ferrure de volet *f*

shutter opener ouvre-volet *m*

shutter retaining hook crémaillère *f*

shutter stay arrêt de volet entrebâilleur *m*

shutter stay (with handle) arrêt de volet avec poignée *m*

signal transmitter, wireless (alarm) transmetteur de signal sans fil *m*

slider coulisse *f*

sliding stay with adjustable stop coulisseau à frein réglable *m*

small case mallette *f*

smoke detector détecteur de fumée *m*

spike broche *f*

spiral spring ressort à boudin *m*

stake piquet *m*

striking plate (lock) gâche *f*

superglue colle universelle instantanée *f*

superglue with brush applicator colle universelle instantanée, 'easy brush' flacon *f*

support support *m*

T-clamp agrafe à T *f*

T-iron profilé en T *m*

threaded stem (door handle) tige filetée *f*

toggle fixing for ceiling cheville en acier à bascule *f*; **(with suspension hook)** ~ avec crochet pour éclairage et suspension *f*; **(with suspension eye)** ~ avec piton pour éclairage et suspension *f*; **(with suspension screw)** ~ avec vis pour éclairage et suspension *f*

toilet brush balai-toilette *m*

toilet roll holder porte-rouleau *m*

toilet seat abattant (d'un siège-toilette) *m*

tool belt ceinture porte-outil *f*

tool box coffre à outils *m*; boîte à outils *f*

tool box, builder's coffre de chantier fixe *m*

tool box, wheeled caisse à outils sur roulettes *f*

tool roll trousse *f*

tool storage rangement des outils *m*

tool storage cupboard, metal armoire de rangement métal *f*

tool wall hook crochet porte-outils *m*

toolboard wall panel panneau mural alvéolé *m*

toolchest, reinforced cantine renforcée *f*

trolley, wheeled chariot à roulettes *m*

tumbler (lock) gorge *f*

video monitor moniteur video *m*

video surveillance vidéo surveillance *m*

wall anchor, hollow cheville métallique à expansion *f*

wall tool rack, magnetic porte-outils magnétique *m*

wallplug cheville *f*

wallplug, cast iron cheville en fonte *f*

wallplug, universal cheville universelle *f*

washer rondelle *f*

washer, flat rondelle plate *f*

washer, large rondelle carrossier *f*

washer, serrated rondelle à denture *f*

washer, split rondelle Grower *f*

weatherstrip bourrelet *m*; joint de calfeutrage *m*

weatherstrip, adhesive PVC (doors and windows) joint adhésif portes et fenêtres PVC *m*

weatherstrip, adhesive rubber P-profile joint adhésif caoutchouc profil «P» *m*

weatherstrip, E-profile joint adhésif caoutchouc profil «E» *m*

weatherstrip, foam joint mousse universel *m*

weatherstrip, grooved (windows) joint fenêtres petites rainures *m*

weatherstrip, long-lasting adhesive foam joint adhésif longue durée combles *m*

window catch crémone *f*

wireless home alarm system kit kit alarme sans fil *m*

NOTES

METALWORK

FERRONNERIE

METALWORK
ENGINEERING
MECHANICS
WELDING

abrasive sheet feuille abrasive *f*

acetylene (gas welding) acétylène *m*

aluminium aluminium *m*

angle grinder meuleuse *f*; ~ d'angle *f*

angle grinder backing pad plateau pour disques *m*

angle grinder cutting stand support tronçonnage de meuleuse *m*

angle iron cornière *f*

angle iron, equal cornière égale *f*

angle iron, unequal cornière inégale *f*

anti-spatter spray (MIG welding) spray anti-adhérent *m*

anti-thermic screen (gas welding) écran thermique *m*

arc welder poste de soudage à l'arc *m*

band saw, metal cutting scie à ruban métal *f*

blowtorch lampe à souder *f*

bolt cutters coupe-boulons *mpl*

brass laiton *m*

brazing rod baguette de brasure *f*; ~ de soudure *f*

brazing rod, arc welding baguette de soudure arc *f*

brazing rod, low temperature aluminium brasure aluminium basse température *f*

brazing rod, silver/ phosphorous/copper baguette de brasage cuivre/ phosphore/argent *f*

bronze bronze *m*

buffing wheel disque drap à polir tissu libre *m*

burner brûleur *m*

burner, enveloping brûleur à flamme enveloppante *m*

burner, extra fine point brûleur à pointe super fine *m*

burner, flat beak brûleur à bec plat *m*

burner, large flame brûleur grande flamme *m*

butane butane *m*

calliper pied à coulisse *m*

calliper, digital vernier pied à coulisse digital *m*

calliper, outside spring compas d'épaisseur *m*

calliper, vernier pied à coulisse vernier *m*

centre punch pointeau *m*; ~ de précision *m*

cleaning rag tampon de nettoyage *m*

cold chisel burin de mécanicien *m*

cold rolled-steel section laminé à froid *m*

cold soldering soudure à froid *f*

copper cuivre *m*

corundum paper abrasif corindon *m*

cup lighter (gas welding) allume-brûleur *m*

cutting disk disque à tronçonner *m*

cutting nozzle (gas welding) tête *f*

cutting torch (gas welding) chalumeau coupeur *m*

cylinder trolley (gas welding) chariot *m*

DC inverter (arc welder) redresseur à courant continu DC *m*

disposable gas bottle cartouche jetable *f*

divider, spring compas à pointes sèches *m*

drill perceuse *f*

drill, bench perceuse d'établi *f*

drill bit foret *m*

drill bit, hexagonal shank metal foret métaux queue hexag *m*

drill bit, high speed steel (HSS) foret HSS *m*

drill bit, reduced shank metal foret métaux queue réduite *m*

drill, manual perceuse manuelle *f*

drill press perceuse sur colonne *f*

drill stand support de perçage *m*

ear defenders casque anti-bruit *m*

ear plugs bouchons d'oreille *mpl*; boulequies *fpl*

earth clamp (arc welder) prise de masse *f*

electrode (arc welder/MIG welder) électrode *f*

electrode holder (arc welder) pince porte-électrode *f*

emery paper papier émeri *m*

epoxy resin mastic mastic soudure à froid universel *m*

feeler gauge calibre d'épaisseur *m*

file lime *f*

file, electric lime électrique *f*

file, flat lime plate à main *f*

file, half-round lime mi-ronde *f*

file, mini lime de précision *f*

file, needle lime aiguille *f*

file, round lime ronde *f*

file, saw lime tiers point *f*

file, square lime carrée *f*

flap disk disque à lamelles *m*

flashback arrestor (gas welding) anti-retour pare flame *m*

flux décapant *m*

fluxed electrode (arc welder) électrode enrobée *f*

galvanised steel acier galvanisé *m*

garnet paper garniture *f*

gas gaz *m*

gas bottle, refillable bouteille gaz rechargeable *f*

gas economiser économiseur de gaz *m*

gas flow meter débilitre à colonne *f*

grinder, bench touret à meuler *m*

grinder, bench (with wire wheel) touret à meuler mixte *m*

grinder, pedestal stand socle pour touret *m*

grinding disk/grinding wheel meule *f*

grinding wheel, coarse grain meule gros grain *f*

grinding wheel, fine grain meule grain fin *f*

hacksaw scie à métaux *f*

hacksaw, mini porte-lame *f*

hacksaw with frame scie à métaux monture *f*

hammer -s marteau (*pl* -x) *m*

hammer, ball pein marteau boule 'anglais'/'américain' *m*

hammer, blacksmith's marteau de forgeron *m*

hammer, chipping (welding) marteau à piquer les soudures *m*

hammer, engineer's marteau de mécanicien *m*

hammer, riveting marteau rivoir *m*

hammer, sputter (sheet metal work and coppersmithing) marteau postillon *m*

headsheild, arc/MIG welding masque de soudure arc/MIG *m*

heat gel (gas welding) gel thermique anti-chaleur *m*

hexagonal key clé mâle *f*

hot glue gun pistolet à colle *m*

hot rolled-steel section laminé à chaud *m*

jigsaw scie sauteuse *f*

jigsaw, laser scie sauteuse laser *f*

jigsaw, pendular scie sauteuse pendulaire *f*

lathe cutting tools outils à pastilles carbure démontables *m*

lathe, metal tour à métaux *m*

mallet maillet *m*; masse *f*; massette *f*

mallet, copper (soft metals) maillet cuivre *m*

mallet, plastic-headed (soft metals) maillet à tête plastique *m*

metal métal (*pl* -aux) *m*

metal bar barre en métal *f*

metal bar, round barre ronde serrurier *f*

metal, ferrous métal ferreux *m*

metal, non-ferrous métal non-ferreux *m*

metal sheet tôle *f*

metal sheet, galvanised tôle galvanisée *f*

metal sheet, perforated tôle perforée *f*

MIG contact tip tube contact vissé *m*

MIG pliers pince MIG *f*

MIG torch torche MIG *f*

MIG welder poste à soudage MIG *m*

MIG welder, gasless poste de soudage à l'arc sans gaz *m*

milling machine fraiseuse *f*

multi-purpose tool pince multifonctions *f*

nickel nickel *m*

nickel-plating nickelage *m*

nickel-silver nickel-argent *m*

oil, hydraulic huile hydraulique *f*

oil, soluble huile soluble *f*

oxygen oxygène *m*

panel beater batte de tôlier-carrossier *f*

pincers tenaille *f*; pince coupante devant de longueur *f*

pincers, mechanic's pince coupante mécanicien *f*

pipe wrench, adjustable pince multiprise réglable *f*

pliers pince *f*

pliers, bent nose pince à becs coudés éffilés *f*

pliers, flat long nose pince à becs plats *f*

pliers, linesman pince universelle de longueur *f*

pliers, long nose pince à bec demi-rond de longueur *f*

pliers, long nose, lock grip pince-étaux bec longs *f*

pliers, round nose pince à becs ronds *f*

pliers, short nose, lock grip pince-étaux bec courts *f*

pliers, side cutting pince coupante de coté de longueur *f*

pliers, water pump pince multiprise de longueur *f*

polishing disk, sisal disque sisal *m*

polishing paste pâte à polir *f*

propane propane *m*

protective apron tablier de protection pour soudure à l'arc *m*

protractor rapporteur d'angle échancré *m*

punch set, letters and numbers lettres et chiffres à frapper *f*

quickfit connectors (gas welding) raccord rapide *m*

reamer head (gas welding) tête à aleser *f*

reamer tools outils pour tête à aleser *m*

rectifier (arc welder) générateur *m*

regulating tap robinet relais *m*

regulator détendeur *m*

rule, flexible stainless steel réglet inox flexible *m*

rule, stainless steel (graduated both sides) réglet semi-rigides inox *m*

silicon carbide paper abrasif carbure de silicium *m*

saw scie *f*

saw blade lame de scie *f*

saw blade, band lame pour scie à ruban métal *f*

saw blade, cut-off lame pour tronçonneuse métal *f*

saw, circular (for metal) scie circulaire métal *f*

saw, cut-off tronçonneuse metal *f*

saw, keyhole ergoscie *f*

saw, sabre scie sabre *f*

scriber pointe à tracer *f*

screwdriver, magnetic tip tournevis lame magnétique *m*

shroud (MIG welder) buse *f*

side cutters pince coupante diagonale *f*

soldering gun, electric pistolet à souder *m*

soldering iron, electric fer à souder électronique *m*

soldering lance lance de soudage *f*

spanner clé *f*

spanner, adjustable; monkey wrench clé à molette *f*

spanner, box or socket clé à pipe *f*; douille *f*

spanner, combination clé mixte *f*

spanner, through box clé à pipe débouchée *f*

speed wrench clé cliquet *f*

square équerre simple à 90° (quatre-vingt-dix degrés) *f*

square, aluminium équerre alu *f*

square section iron carré *f*

square, steel équerre acier *f*

stainless steel inox *m*

stand, bench grinder support touret à meuler *m*

star key clé étoile *f*

steel acier *m*

tap and die set coffret de tarauds et filières *m*

tape measure mètre ruban *m*

tee section, equal té à ailes égales *m*

tin solder soudure étain *f*

tin solder, bobbin of bobine de souder soudure étain *f*

toolbox, mechanic's caisse mécanicien *f*

torch, gas chalumeau monogaz *m*

torch, gas welding chalumeau *m*

torch, heating chalumeau chauffeur *m*

torch hose, small bore manchette équipée *f*

torch, pencil flame stylo soudeur gaz *m*

torch, welding, soldering, cutting chalumeau *m*

tube tube *m*

tube, rectangular hollow section tube métal rectangulaire *m*

tube, round metal tube rond *m*

tube, square hollow section tube carré *m*

U-shaped channel U à conge *m*

vice étau *m*

welding, arc soudure a l'arc *f*

welding blanket pare flame *f*

welding, gas soudure gaz *f*

welding gauntlet gant spécial pour soudure à l'arc *m*

welding goggles lunettes de soudage *f*; ~ de protection *f*

welding hose tuyau *m*

welding kit, two gases chalumeau bi-gaz *m*

welding, MIG soudure MIG *f*

welding nozzle buse de soudage *f*

welding rod baguette de métal d'apport et étain *f*

welding table table de soudage *f*

welding tools outils de soudure *m*

welding torch chalumeau soudeur *m*

whet stone grinder meule à eau *f*

wire fil *m*

wire, gasless MIG, fil fourré acier sans gaz *m*

wire, gasless MIG (on bobbin) bobine fourré pour poste sans gaz *f*

wire, MIG welding (on bobbin) bobine fourré *f*

wire, mild steel fil acier *m*

wire, solid fil massif *m*

zinc sheet, electroplated tôle electrozinguée *f*

NOTES

PLUMBING & HEATING

PLOMBERIE & CHAUFFAGE

abrasive agent décapant *m*

access plug bouchon fileté *m*

air bubble bulle d'air *f*

air pocket poche d'air *f*

air vent ventouse *f* **align, to** aligner *v*

aluminium aluminium *m*

anti-hardwater device, magnetic anti-calcaire magnétique *m*; **(for showers)** ~ pour la douche *m*; **(for washing machines/ dishwashers)** ~ pour machine à laver et lave-vaisselle *m*

anti-hardwater silico- phosphate balls billes silico- phosphate anti-calcaire *m*

anti-pollution valve clapet anti-pollution *m*

antivibration antivibratile *adj*

ball valve vanne *f*

ball valve (alongside meter) vanne pour compteur *f*

ball valve, T-type vanne à sphère raccords bicônes *f*

ball valve, tap vanne à sphère *f*

ball valve, through vanne à passage intégral *f*

ball valve with butterfly tap vanne papillon *f*

ball valve with hose connector, tap vanne à sphère puisage *f*

ball valve with purge, tap vanne à sphère avec purges *f*

basin lavabo *m*; cuvette *f*

bath baignoire *f*

bath, hip- baignoire sabot *f*

bath, hydrotherapy baignoire à bulle *f*

bend, pipe coude de tube *m*

bend, S- coude de renvoi

bend, U- coude en U *m*

bibcock robinet *m* (nearest equivalent)

bidet bidet *m*

blowlamp/blowtorch chalumeau (*pl* -x) *m*; lampe à souder *f*

blowlamp/blowtorch cup lighter allume-brûleur *m*

blowtorch, cutting (oxy- acetylene or oxy-propane) chalumeau soudeur *m*

blowtorch, gas (butane or propane) chalumeau monogaz *m*

boiler chaudière *f*

boiler, connection kit kit de raccordement universel pour chaudière *m*

boiler, floor-standing chaudière au sol *f*; **(with hot water tank)** ~ avec ballon *f*

boiler flue carneau de chaudière *m*

boiler, gas chaudière gaz *f*

boiler, oil chaudière fioul *f*; **(with hot water tank)** ~ production d'eau chaude par ballon *f*

boiler, wall-mounted chaudière murale *f*; **(without hot water tank)** ~ sans ballon *f*; **(with hot water tank)** ~ avec ballon *f*

bowl cuvette *f*

braze, to braser *v*

brazing rod baguette de brasure *f*

burner, gas brûleur gaz *m*

burner, oil brûleur fioul *m*

butane (gas) butane *m*

cesspool fosse d'aisances *f*

circulating pump, three-speed circulateur trois vitesse *f*

cistern citerne *f*

clean, to nettoyer *v*

cleaning rag tampon de nettoyage *m*

cleaning rod baguette de nettoyage *f*

cock robinet à boisseau *m*

cold water storage cistern no equivalent; French systems are sealed

conduit gaine *f*

connector joint *m*

connector, equal tee té égal *m*

connector, reducing réduction *f*; manchon dilation *m*

connector, straight coulisse *f*

connector, straight male to female manchette réparation *f*

connector without lip, straight manchon sans lèvre *m*

conversion bend coude à joint *m*

corrode, to corroder *v*

corrosion corrosion *f*

counterflow contre-courant *m*

cylinder cylindre *m*

de-limescaling powder for washing machines and dishwashers poudre détartrante et dégraissante pour lave-linge et lave-vaisselle *f*

die head tête de filère *f*

discharge décharge *f*

disconnect débrancher *v*

disinfection désinfection *f*

drain égout *m*

drain clearing tool
déboucheur *m*

**drain clearing tool, cranked
spring** déboucheur fléxible à
manivele *m*; ~ à crampons *m*

drain clearing tool, piston
déboucheur à piston *m*

drain clearing tool, pump
pompe à vide *f*

drain clearing tool, spool
déboucheur à tambour *m*

drain off, to vidanger *v*

drain, to vider *v*

drainage system système de
drainage *m*

draincock purgeur à bec *m*; ~
équerre *m*

drainpipe tuyau d'écoulement *m*

drinking water eau buvable *f*

drip, to égoutter *v*

duct conduite *f*

expansion bottle vase
d'expansion sanitaire *f*

file lime *f*

filter mesh grille du filtre *f*

fixed bridge clamp collier à
crémaillère à vis *m*

flange collet *m*

flue cheminée *f*

flux flux décapant *m*

galvanise, to galvaniser *v*

gas gaz *m*

gas, disposable bottle cartouche
jetable *f*

gas, natural gaz naturel *m*

gas pipe tuyau à gaz *m*

**gas pipe, flexible (natural
gas)** tuyau flexible pour gaz
naturel *m*

gas, refillable bottle bouteille
gaz rechargeable *f*

gas regulating tap robinet
relais gaz *m*

gas regulator détendeur *m*

gas tap, push and turn robinet
pousser/tourner *m*

gasket joint d'étanchéité *m*

**grease trap (for drainage
system)** bac dégraisseur *m*

gully, rainwater regard de
branchement pour eaux
pluviales *m*

gutter gouttière *f*

hacksaw scie à métaux *f*

hard water neutraliser
neutraliseur de calcaire *f*

heat, to chauffer *v*

heater réchauffeur *m*

heating chauffage *m*

heating, back-up chauffage d'appoint *m*

heating, central chauffage centrale *m*

heating, gas chauffage au gaz *m*

heating, oil chauffage au fioul *m*

hole-making punch emporte-pièce *m*

hose clip collier *m*

hose clip, ratcheted collier à crémaillère *m*

hosepipe tuyau d'arrosage *m*

hot water tank ballon d'eau chaude *m*

impermeable imperméable *adj*

inlet admission *f*; entrée *f*

inlet pipe tuyau d'entrée *m*

insulate, to isoler *v*

insulation isolation *f*

joint, copper raccord cuivre *m*

joint, copper soldered (capillary fitting) raccord cuivre à souder *m*

joint, soldered angle raccord courbe cuivre à souder *m*

joint, soldered elbow raccord coude cuivre à souder *m*

joint, soldered equal tee raccord té cuivre à souder égal *m*

joint, soldered reducing tee raccord té cuivre à souder réduction *m*

joint, soldered tee raccord té cuivre à souder *m*

joint stop end, brass soldered bouchon laiton à souder *m*

joint, straight soldered manchon cuivre à souder *m*

joint with olive, brass compression raccord à olive *m*

leak; leakage fuite *f*

leak detector détecteur de fuites *m*

limescale filter, washing machine filtre anti-tartre pour machine à laver *m*

macerator pompe de relevage *f*

manhole regard *m*

manometer manomètre *m*

mastic, leak repair mastique à réparer les fuites *m*

MDPE blue water pipe tuyau polyéthylène eau potable *m*

overflow trop-plein *m*

meter compteur *m*; débordement *m*

meter, volume compteur de volume *m*

meter, water compteur d'eau froide *m*

outlet décharge *f*

pipe tuyau *m*; canalisation *f*

pipe bend coude de tube *m*

pipe bending spring ressort à cintrer *m*

pipe bending tool malette cintreuse *f*; pince à cintrer *f*

pipe clip collier simple *m*

pipe clip, conical black plate rosace conique *f*

pipe clip, flat back plate rosace plate *f*

pipe, copper tuyau cuivre *m*

pipe cutter coupe-tube *m*

pipe cutter blade, replacement molette pour coupe-tube cuivre *f*

pipe cutter, copper coupe-tube cuivre *f* *(see also: tube cutter)*

pipe, hand-bendable tuyau flexible d'alimentation souple *m*

pipe, overflow tuyau de trop-plein

pipe, PVC (plastic, polyvinylchloride) tuyau PVC *m*

pipe seal cord fil d'étanchéité bobine *m*

pipe sealing tape, rubber ruban caoutchouc pour colmatage *m*

pipe wrench serre-tubes *m*

pipeline (gas) canalisation de gaz *f*

pipework canalisation *f*

pipework, plastic canalisation en plastique *f*

pipework, plastic waste canalisations d'évacuation en plastique *f*

piping tubulure *f*

pliers pince *f* *(see also: spanner; wrench)*

pliers, adjustable wide jaw pince à siphon *f*; ~ griptou *f*

pliers, plumber's; ~ tube tightening clé Suédoise *f*; serre-tubes Suédoise *f*

plug bonde *f*

plughole and plug bonde à bouchon *f*

plumb, to plomber *v*

plumber's workshop plomberie *f*

plumbing plomberie *f*

plumbline plomb *m*

pressure pression *f*

pressure reducer réducteur de pression *m*

pressure reducer, water heater réducteur de pression spécial chauffe-eau *m*

pressure reducing valve détendeur *m*

pressure regulator écrêteur *m*

programmer, heating cassette de programmation *f*

propane (gas) propane *m*

PTFE joint sealing tape ruban Téflon d'étanchéité *m*

pump, circulating pompe de circulation *f*

pump, electric pompe électrique *f*

pump, heat pompe à chaleur *f*

purge, to; purify, to épurer *v*

purification épuration *f*

PVC solvent-weld adhesive colle PVC *f*

radiator radiateur *m*

radiator bleed key clé purgeur à radiateur *f*

radiator bleed valve purgeur automatique pour radiateur *m*

radiator bleed valve, automatic purgeur pour radiateur *m*

radiator head tool clé de montage de radiateur *f*

radiator tap robinet de radiateur *m*

radiator, towel radiateur sèche-serviette *m*

radiator valve, thermostatic robinet de radiateur à tête thermostatique *m*

radiator, water-filled radiateur à eau *m*

reducing connector, off-centre réduction excentrée *f*

regulate, to régler *v*

regulator régulateur *m*

reservoir réservoir *m*

rubber caoutchouc *m*

sanitary sanitaire *adj*

sanitation assainissement *m*

scale incrustations *fpl*

scale deposit encroûtement *m*

scale inhibitor, electronic anti-tartre électronique *f*

scour, to décrasser *v*

seal joint d'étanchéité *m*

seal off, to colmater *v*

security valves groupe de sécurité *m*

sediment sédiment *m*

septic tank fosse septique *f*; ~ 'toutes eaux' *f*

sewage eaux usées *fpl*

sewage, raw eaux d'égout brutes *fpl*

sewage system système du tout à l'égout *m*

sewer égout *m*

shower douche *f*

shower cabinet cabine de douche *f*

shower rose douchette *f*

shower screen pare-douche *m*

shower trap bonde de douche *f*

shower tray receveur de douche *m*

shower tray, floor-mounted bac à poser *m*

shower tray, inset receveur à encaster *m*

shower tray, raised receveur surélevé *m*

sink évier *m*

siphon siphon *m*

smoke pipe conduit fumée *f*

socket forming tool outil universel pour emboitement *m*

soil pipe saddle selle tuyau *f*

solder fil de soudure *m*; ~ d'étain à braser *m*

solder, to braser *v*; souder *v*

solder wire fil de soudure *m*

soldering soudage *m*; soudure *f*; soudure à la flame *f*

soldering lance lance de soudage *f*

soldering nozzle buse de soudage *f*

soldering nozzle, enveloping brûleur à flamme enveloppante *m*

soldering nozzle, extra fine point brûleur à pointe super fine *m*

soldering nozzle, flat beak brûleur à bec plat *m*

soldering nozzle, large flame brûleur grande flamme *m*

spanner clé *f (see also: pliers; wrench)*

spanner, adjustable clé à molette *f*

stopcock robinet d'arrêt *m*

stoptap robinet d'arrêt *m*

stoptap with drain valve robinet d'arrêt avec purge *m*

stoptap with hose connector robinet de puisage *m*

stoptap without drain valve robinet d'arrêt à raccord sans purge *m*

stopvalve vanne d'arrêt *f*

tap robinet *m*

tap connector raccord tourant bicone *m*

tap, cross-head robinet manette crosillon *m*

tap head tête de robinet *f*

tap kit and filter kit robinet
et filter *m*

tap, mixer mélangeur *m*;
mitigeur *m*

tap, outside robinet extérieur *m*

tap, push robinet poussoir *m*

tap, self-cutting robinet
autoperceur *m*

tap, separate control robinet à
commande unique *m*

tap washer joint de robinet *m*

tap with temperature control
mitigeur thermostatique *m*

taps robinetterie *f*

tee piece té pied biche *m*

**telephone remote control
(heating control)**
télécommande téléphonique
vocale *f*

thermostat thermostat *m*

thermostat, electronic
thermostat électronique *m*

thermostat, high precision
thermostat de haute précision *m*

thermostat, mechanical
thermostat mécanique *m*

thermostat, programmable
thermostat programmable *m*

**thermostat, radio/telephone
control** thermostat

électronique programmable
radio/tél *m*

toilet WC *mpl*; vécés *mpl*

toilet bowl cuvette *f*

trap siphon *m (see also: waste trap)*

trap, bottle siphon canal net *m*;
siphon à culot *m*

trap, multi-position sink
siphon évier multi-positions *m*

trap, sink/washing machine
siphon évier *m*; prise machine
à laver *m*

tube, copper tube de cuivre *m*; ~
cuivre écroui *m*; tuyau de cuivre *m*
(see also: pipe)

tube, CPVC tube en PVC-C *m*

tube cutter coupe-tube *f (see
also: pipe cutter)*

tube, microbore (in coil)
cuivre recuit (en couronne) *m*

upstand siphon avec tube
droit *m*

valve soupape *f*

wall plate elbow applique
murale *f*

washbasin lavabo *m*; lave-mains
m; vasque *f*

washer joint de raccord *m*

washer, CSC (hot water) joint
CSC pour eau chaude *m*

washer, fibre (cold water) joint fibre pour eau froide *m*

washer, rubber (manual tightening) joint caoutchouc serrage manuel *m*

washing machine machine à laver *f*

washing machine drain hose, extendable canne de vidange extensible *f*

washing machine drain hose, Y piece embout alimentation en 'Y' *m*

washing machine waste outlet kit prise de vidange universel *m*

waste outlet system système de vidange *m*

waste to soil pipe adapter tampon de réduction *m*

waste to soil pipe adapter, double tampon double *m*

waste pipe canalisation vidange *f*

waste pipe connector raccord vidange *m*

waste pipe connector, washbasin raccord sortie lavabo *m*

waste pipe, flexible raccord d'évacuation souple *m*

waste trap siphon *m*

waste trap, washbasin/bidet siphon gain de place lavabo/bidet *m*

water eau *f*

water butt réservoir d'eau *m*

water heater chauffe-eau *m*

water heater, electric (equiv. immersion heater) chauffe-eau électrique *m*

water heater, instantaneous gas chauffe-eau gaz instantané *m*

water heater, solar chauffe-eau solaire *m*

water filter filtrante de l'eau *f*

water filter bypass system kit kit bypass pour filtre *m*

water filter cartridge cartouche filtrante *f*

water filter cartridge, replacement cartouche de rechange *f*

water filter jug carafe filtrante *f*

water level niveau de l'eau *m*

water meter compteur d'eau froide *m*

water softener adoucisseur d'eau *m*

water softener disinfectant désinfectant pour adoucisseurs *m*

water softener regenerating salt sel régénerant pour adoucisseur d'eau *m*

water softener salt tablets pastilles de sel pour adoucisseur d'eau *f*

water treatment traitement de l'eau *m*

water treatment centre centrale de traitement d'eau *m*

water treatment unit unité de traitment d'eau *m*

watertight étanchéité *f*

weld, to souder *v*

welding soudure autogène *f*; ~ à la flame *f*

welding blanket pare flamme *m*

welding goggles lunettes de soudage *fpl*

welding hose tuyau *m*

welding kit poste à souder *f*

welding kit, two gases chalumeau bi-gaz *f*

welding nozzle buse de soudage *f*

welding rod baguette de métal d'apport et étain *f*

wrench clé *f (see also: spanner; pliers)*

wrench, adjustable clé à molette *f*

wrench, basin clé lavabo *f*

wrench, chain clé à chaine *f*

wrench, monkey clé anglaise *f*

wrench, plumber's clé Suédoise *f*

wrench, Stillson clé Stillson *f*

NOTES

PROPERTY

PROPRIETE

HOUSES
BUILDINGS
ROOMS
LANDSCAPE
PURCHASE
LEGAL

acre not used in France; equivalent: hectare (approx. 2½ acres) *m*

advance deposit on purchase arrhes *fpl*

agreement authorising estate agent to search for property mandat de recherche *m*

agreement to sell mandat de vente *m*

apartment block; block of flats maison de rapport *f*

apartment, furnished maison meublée *f*

attestation; affidavit attestation *f*

attic grenier *m*; comble *m*

auction vente aux enchères *f*

bank account, non-interest accruing (used by notaire for deposits) caisse des dépots et consignations *f*

barn grange *f*

barn for straw pailler *m*

basement sous-sol *m*

bathroom salle de bain *f*

bedroom chambre *f*

birth certificate acte de naissance *m*

Breton stone-built farmhouse; long house longère *f*

boundary limite du terrain *f*

building land terrain à bâtir *m*

bungalow bungalow *m*; pavillon *m*

buyer; purchaser acheteur -euse *mf*

cancellation of contract résiliation *f*

capital gains tax plus-value *f*

carport abri *m*; ~ voiture *m*

cash payment paiement comptant *m*

cellar cave *f*

certificate equivalent to a local authority search certificat d'urbanisme *m*

certified copy of notarial document expédition *f*

communal parts of a building parties communes *fpl*

conditional terms in a pre-sale agreement conditions suspensives *fpl*

conservatory véranda *f*

conveyance of land transfer; deed of sale acte de vente *m*; ~ authentique de vente *m*; ~ d'achat *m*

co-ownership copropriété *f*

copse taillis *m*

cottage cottage *m*

cowshed; cattleshed; byre
étable *f*

death certificate acte de décès *m*

deposit acompte *m*

dining room salle à manger *f*

ditch fossé *m*

drainage système
d'assainissement *m*

entrance hall vestibule *m*

family room salle de séjour *f*

**farm, small; country/weekend
cottage** fermette *f*

fence barrière *f*; cloture *f*

field champ *m*

financing scheme plan de
financement *m*

flooding inondations *fpl*

for rent à louer *adj*

for sale à vendre *adj*

**funds supplied by flat-
owners to meet unexpected
liabilities** fonds de
roulement *mpl*

garage garage *m*

gatekeeper's lodge maisonette
du garde *f*

**good for acquisition (phrase
written accompanying
signature of contract)** bon
pour achat *expr (see also: read
and approved)*

granary grenier *m*

hill colline *f*

hilly accidenté *adj*

**house; home; abode;
residence** maison *f*

house and land purchase achat
de maison et terrain *m*

house, country maison de
campagne *f*

house, country manor
gentilhommière *f*

house, dwelling maison
d'habitation *f*

house, farm- ferme *f*; maison
paysanne *f*

house, gentleman's maison de
maître *f*

house, Provençal country
bastide *f*

**house, Provençal farm (low,
L-shaped)** mas *m*

house, suburban maison de
banlieue *f*

house, town maison de ville *f*

house, weekend/holiday
maison de plaisance *f*;
résidence secondaire *f*; ~
d'amis *f*

housing estate; plot of land lotissement *m*

hunting lodge maison de chasse *f*

inheritance/gift tax droit de succession/donation *m*

joint ownership indivision *f*

joint ownership tontine *f*

junk room débarras *m*

kitchen cuisine *f*

land designated for building terrain constructible *m*

landowner propriétaire *mf*

land registry cadastre *m*

land registry plot applied in an apartment block lot *m*

larder garde-manger *m*

laundry buanderie *f (see also: utility room)*

law protecting borrowers (from French lenders and sellers on French property purchases) loi scrivener *f*

lease to tenant bail *m*

let-out clause clause suspensive *f*

level crossing keeper's cottage maisonette de garde-barrière *f*

library bibliothèque *f*

life interest jouissance *f*

listed building monument historique *m*

living room salon *m*

mansion maison bourgeoise *f*

marriage certificate extrait d'acte de mariage *m*

marshland marais *m*

mortgage in which property is used as loan security hypothèque *f*

mortgage/land registry conservation des hypothèques *f*

non-binding offer to buy or sell property offre d'achat *f*; offre de vente *f*

notarial certificate (confirming completion of property purchase) attestation d'acquisition *f*

notary's scale of charges émoluments *mpl*

office bureau *m*

outbuilding; part of a farm dépendance *f*

ownership without usufruct (in which purchaser has no occupational rights over a property until death or prior surrender

of life tenant) nue-
propriété *f*
**parts of building restricted
solely to use of owner** parties
privatives *fpl*
path chemin *m*
penalty clause clause pénale *f*
pigeon tower pigeonnier *m*
pigsty porcherie *f*
planning permission permis de
construire *m*
post, fence piquet de clôture *f*
power of attorney procuration *f*
**pre-emptive right (to
acquire property instead
of purchaser)** droit de
préemption *m*
pre-sale agreement, private
acte sous seing privé *m*
property deed acte notarié *m*
**proportion of communal
parts of a co-ownership
with other apartment
owners** tantième *m*
pond étang *m*
**purchase agreement; contract
of sale** compromis de vente *m*
purchase contract contrat
de réservation *m*; contrat
préliminaire *m*

pylon pylône *m*
**read and approved (phrase
written accompanying
signature of contract)** lu et
approuvé *expr (see also: good for
acquisition)*
receipt reçu *m*
**registration of title
of ownership** droits
d'enregistrement *m*
rental; lease location *f*
**residency permit
(discontinued)** carte de séjour
f; permis de séjour *m*
**rest home; convalescent
home** maison de repos *f*; ~ de
convalescence *f*
retirement home maison de
retraite *f*
revenue stamp timbre fiscal *m*
**schedule of condition/
delapidations (beginning or
end of lease)** états des lieux *m*
sea level niveau de la mer *m*
semi-detached houses maisons
doubles *fpl*
sheep farm bergerie *f*
slope pente *f*
small house; cottage
maisonette *f*

spring source *f*

square kilometre kilomètre
carré *m*

stable (for horse) écurie *f*

**sum paid to notary (including
sale price, notary's fee,
registration duty, land
registration duty and other
charges)** frais de notaire *mpl*

telegraph pole poteau
télégraphique *m*

thatched cottage chaumière *f*

utility room buanderie *f (see also:
laundry)*

vendor; seller vendeur -euse *mf*

will testament *m*

wine warehouse chai *m*

workshop atelier *m*

NOTES

TRADES

METIERS

ambulance driver ambulancier
-ère *mf*

architect architecte *mf*

blacksmith forgeron *m*

bricklayer maçon *m*

builder constructeur *m*

cabinet maker ébéniste *mf*

carpenter charpentier *m*

caterer traiteur *m*

cattleman éleveur *m*

cesspool cleaner vidangeur *m*

chartered accountant expert-
comptable *m*

chimneysweep ramoneur *m*

computer specialist
informaticien -enne *mf*;
informatique *f*

consultant expert-conseil *m*

craftsman/woman artisan -e *mf*

**diagnostic professional
(e.g. testing for lead and
asbestos)** expert immobilier *m*

doctor docteur *m*

doctor, medical medécin *m*

draughtsman/woman
dessinateur -trice *mf*

electrician électricien *m*

estate agent agent immobilier *m*

**expert (architect or other,
licensed to check state and
value of property)** expert
foncier *m*

farmer agriculteur -trice *mf*

fireman pompier *m*; sapeur-
pompier *m*

foreman/woman contremaître
-esse *mf*; maître d'oeuvre *m*

gardener jardinier -ière *mf*

glazier vitrier *m*

handyman/woman bricoleur
-euse *mf*

hardware merchant
quincaillier -ière *mf*

heating specialist chauffagiste *m*

horticulturist horticulteur
-trice *mf*

insurance agent agent
d'assurance *m*

iron craftsman ferronnier
-ière *mf*

interior decorator tapissier
décorateur *m*

joiner menuisier *m*

labourer travailleur -euse *mf*

landscape gardener
paysagiste *mf*

landscape labourer terrassier
- ière *mf*

lawyer avocat -e *mf*

locksmith serrurier -ière *mf*

market gardener maraîcher -ère *mf*

mechanic/service station worker garagiste *mf*

mutual insurance company mutuelle *f*

notary notaire *m*

nurseryman pépiniériste *mf*

painter peintre *m*

plasterer plâtrier *m*

plumber plombier *m*

policeman policier *m*; gendarme *m (see also: police officer)*

police officer officier de police *m (see also: policeman)*

property dealer marchand -e de biens *mf*

quantity surveyor; supervisor métreur -euse *mf*

quarryman cariste *m*

removal company déménageur *m*

roofer couvreur *m*

secretary secrétaire *mf*

shopkeeper; tradesman/ woman marchand -e *mf*

surveyor géomètre *mf*; arpenteur -euse *mf*

upholsterer tapissier -ière *mf*

veterinarian vétérinaire *mf*

workforce mains-d'oeuvre *m*

workman/worker ouvrier -ière *mf*

zinc-roofer plombier-zinguer *m*

NOTES

NUMBERS

LES NOMBRES

NUMBERS
FRACTIONS
DECIMALS
PERCENTAGES

0 nought zéro	**30 thirty** trente
1 one un (une)	**40 forty** quarante
2 two deux	**50 fifty** cinquante
3 three trois	**60 sixty** soixante
4 four quatre	**70 seventy** soixante-dix
5 five cinq	**71 seventy-one** soixante et onze
6 six six	**72 seventy-two** soixante-douze
7 seven sept	**80 eighty** quatre-vingts
8 eight huit	**81 eighty-one** quatre-vingt-un
9 nine neuf	(une)
10 ten dix	**90 ninety** quatre-vingt-dix
11 eleven onze	**91 ninety-one** quatre-vingt-onze
12 twelve douze	**100 a hundred** cent
13 thirteen treize	**101 a hundred and one** cent un
14 fourteen quatorze	**200 two hundred** deux cents
15 fifteen quinze	**201 two hundred and one**
16 sixteen seize	deux cent un (une)
17 seventeen dix-sept	**300 three hundred** trois cents
18 eighteen dix-huit	**1,000 a thousand** mille
19 nineteen dix-neuf	**1,000,000 a million** un million
20 twenty vingt	
21 twenty-one vingt et un (une)	**1st first** 1er premier -ière
22 twenty-two vingt-deux	**2nd second** 2e / 2ème deuxième
23 twenty-three vingt-trois	**3rd third** 3e / 3ème troisième
24 twenty-four vingt-quatre	**4th fourth** 4e / 4ème quatrième
25 twenty-five vingt-cinq	**5th fifth** 5e / 5ème cinquième
26 twenty-six vingt-six	**6th sixth** 6e / 6ème sixième
27 twenty-seven vingt-sept	**7th seventh** 7e / 7ème septième
28 twenty-eight vingt-huit	**8th eighth** 8e / 8ème huitième
29 twenty-nine vingt-neuf	**9th ninth** 9e / 9ème neuvième

10th tenth 10e / 10ème dixième
11th eleventh 11e / 11ème
onzième
12th twelfth 12e / 12ème douzième
13th thirteenth 13e / 13ème
treizième
14th fourteenth 14e / 14ème
quatorzième
15th fifteenth 15e / 15ème
quinzième
16th sixteenth 16e / 16ème
seizième
17th seventeenth 17e / 17ème dix-
septième
18th eighteenth 18e / 18ème dix-
huitième
19th nineteenth 19e / 19ème dix-
neuvième
20th twentieth 20e / 20ème
vingtième
21st twenty-first 21e / 21ème
vingt-et-unième
30th thirtieth 30e / 30ème
trentième
100th hundredth 100e / 100ème
centième
101st hundred-and-first 101e /
101ème cent-unième
1,000th thousandth 1,000^e /
1,000^{ème} millième

FRACTIONS LES FRACTIONS
a half un demi
a third un tiers
two-thirds deux tiers
a quarter un quart
a fifth un cinquième

DECIMALS LES DECIMAUX
0.5 nought point five 0,5 zéro
virgule cinq

PERCENTAGES
POURCENTAGE
5% five per cent 5% cinq pour
cent
100% one hundred per cent
100% cent pour cent

NOTES

MAÇONNERIE

BUILDING

CONSTRUCTION
ROOFING
INSULATION
DAMP-PROOFING
PLASTERING
DRAINAGE

abouter *v* to abut

absorber *v* to absorb

accélérateur *m* accelerator

accélérateur rapid *m* set accelerator

accessoire *m* accessory

achever *v* to end (work)

acier *m* steel

additif *m* additive

adhérence *f* adhesion

adhérer *v* to adhere

adjuvant *m* additive

adjuvant accélérateur antigel *m* mortar and concrete cold temperature accelerator additive

adjuvant des mortiers *m* mortar and concrete additive

adjuvant fibres synthétiques *m* mortar and concrete reinforcing additive

adjuvant hydrofuge *m* mortar and concrete water repellent additive

adjuvant plastifiant *m* mortar and concrete plasticiser additive

adjuvant pour bétonnage par temps froid *m* concrete antifreeze additive

agent de démoulage *m* concrete mould release agent

agent entraîneur d'air *m* concrete air entraining agent

aggloméré (agglo *abbr***)** *m* chipboard

agrafe *f* clamp

agrafeuse *f* staple gun

agrandir *v* to enlarge

agrandissement *m* extension

agrégat *m* aggregate

alcôve *f* alcove

alène *f* awl

aligner *v* to align

alimentation en gaz *f* gas supply

aménagement *m* conversion

aménager *v* to convert; to develop

ancien -enne *adj* ancient

ancre *f* anchor

ancrer *v* to anchor; to fix

annexe *f* annexe

anti-humidité *adj* anti-humidity

antirouille *adj* antirust

appareil *m* appliance; machinery

appartement *m* apartment

appentis *m* lean-to

architecte *m* architect

architrave *f* architrave *(see also: baguette)*

ardoise *f* roofing slate

ardoise fibres-ciment *f* fibre cement roofing slate

arêtier *m* hip rafter

argile *f* clay

argile expansée *f* expanded clay

armature *f* reinforcement

armature à toit *f* roof truss *(see also: ferme de charpente)*

arrière *m* back

aspirateur dynamique éolien *m* chimney flue extractor

aspirateur, eau et poussières *m* vacuum cleaner (water and dust)

assemblage *m* joint

assemblage à clés amovibles *m* keyed joint

assembler *v* to assemble; to join

auge *f* mixing trough

avant-toit *m* eaves *(see also: comble extérieur)*

bac dégraisseur *m* grease trap (for drainage system)

bâche *f* tarpaulin

bâcler *v* to botch

badigeon *m* lime paint; whitewash

badigeonner *v* to whitewash

baguette *f* architrave *(see also: architrave)*

baguette d'angle *f* angle bead

balai *m* broom

balcon *m* balcony

balustrade *f* balustrade

balustre *m* staircase baluster

bande à joint *f* plasterboard jointing tape

bande d'étanchéité *f* flashing strip

bande d'étanchéité indéchirable autocollante *f* self-adhesive tear-resistant flashing strip

bande de solin *f* flashing strip; flaunching

bande renfort d'angle *f* plasterboard corner jointing tape

bardeau (*pl* -x) *m* roof shingle

bardeau (*pl* -x) verrier bitumen *m* bituminous felt roof shingle

base *f* base

bâtard mortier *m* cement/lime mix; lime mortar

bâtiment *m* building

bâtir *v* to build *(see also: construire)*

bêche *f* spade; shovel

benne *f* skip

béton *m* concrete

béton à prise rapide *m* rapid-setting concrete

béton allégé libre *m* lightweight concrete

bétonner *v* to cement *(see also: cimenter)*

bétonneuse *f* cement mixer

bétonnière *f* cement mixer

bilan *m* assessment

biseau *m* bevel

biseauté -e *adj* bevelled

biseauter *v* to bevel

bitume *m* bitumen

bloc à bancher *m* hollow breezeblock (for filling with concrete)

bloc béton cellulaire *m* concrete cellular insulating block

bloc creux *m*; ~ **à bancher** *m* hollow breezeblock (for filling with concrete)

bloc creux en béton *m* hollow concrete block

bloc d'angle *m* pilaster breezeblock (for reinforcement; not available in UK)

bloc linteau *m* lintel block

bloc pilier *m* walling pillar

bloc plein *m* full size breezeblock

bloc plein allégé *m* alleviated breezeblock

bloc plein de granulats *m* solid aggregate block

bloc plein en béton *m* solid conrete block

bloc plein perforé *m* perforated full size breezeblock

bloc U *m* U-shaped channel breezeblock (not available in UK)

blocage *m* blockage

blocaille *f* ballast

boiserie *f* panelling

boîte à outils *f* toolbox

bomber *v* to bulge (e.g. wall)

bord *m* border

bord arrondi *m* nosing (e.g. of a stair tread)

bordurette *f* paving edging

borne *f* boundary stone or marker

boue *f* mud

boulon *m* bolt

bourrelet d'étanchéité *m* angle bead

bride *f* clamp

brider *v* to clamp

brique *f* brick

brique à couteau *f* arch brick

brique auto-isolante en terre cuite *f* cellular terracotta insulating block

brique creuse de terre cuite *f* hollow terracotta brick

brique de pavage *f* paving brick

brique de type courant *f* standard type brick

brique de ventilation *f* ventilation brick

brique de verre *f* glass brick

brique perforée *f* perforated brick

brique pleine *f* full size brick

briqueter *v* to brick

brosse *f* brush

brouette *f* wheelbarrow

câble *m* cable

câble enterré *m* buried cable

cage escalier *f* stairwell

cailloutage *m* pebbledash

calorifugeage *m* lagging

caniveau *m* drainage channel

caniveau en béton *m* concrete drainage channel

caniveau polyester renforcé de fibre de verre *m* glass reinforced plastic drainage channel

carreau (*pl* -x) *m* floor tile; wall tile

carreau alvéolé *m* honeycomb plaster block

carreau de faïence *m* ceramic tile

carreau de plâtre creux *m* hollow plaster block

carreau de plâtre hydrofugé *m* waterproofed plaster block

carreau de terre cuite *m* terracotta tile

carreau plâtre *m* plaster block

carreau plein *m* solid plaster block

carrelage *m* tiling

carrelage en briques *m* brick paving

carreler *v* to tile

cave *m* cellar

cavité *f* cavity

chaînage *m* bonding beam/ girder (reinforcement)

chambranle *m* door or window frame

chantier *m* building site

chape *f* screed

chapeau de cheminée *m* chimney cap

charpente *f* framework

chaume *m* thatch

chasse à pierre *f* chasing chisel

chaux *f* lime

chaux blanche naturelle *f* natural white lime

chaux colorée teintée *f* coloured lime

chaux de Saint Astier *f* St. Astier lime

chaux grise *f* grey lime

chaux hydraulique *f* hydraulic lime

chaux naturelle formulae *f* naturally formulated lime

cheminée *f* chimney; fireplace

cheminée, chapeau de *m* chimney cap

chevillette *f* clamping peg (not available in UK)

chevron *m* rafter

chute *f* drop

ciment *m* cement

ciment à maçonner *m* masonry cement

ciment blanc *m* white cement

ciment blanc multi-usuages *m* all-purpose white cement

ciment colle *m* tile adhesive

ciment fondu *m* heat-resistant cement

ciment gris *m* grey cement

ciment gris multi-usages *m* all-purpose grey cement

ciment hautes performances *m* high-performance cement

ciment joint *m* tile joint cement

ciment milieux aggressifs *m* sulphate-resisting cement

ciment multi-usages *m* all-purpose cement

ciment prêt à l'emploi *m* dry-mixed cement

ciment prompt *m*; ~ **bâti prompt** *m* quick-setting cement

ciment spécial *m* special-purpose cement

ciment super blanc *m* extra-white cement

cimenter *v* to cement *(see also: bétonner)*

cintre *m* curve

cintrer *v* to bend; to curve

ciseau (*pl* -x) *m* chisel -s

ciseau à brique *m* bolster chisel

ciseau de maçon *m* cold chisel

ciseler *v* to chisel

citerne *f* cistern

cloison *f* partition wall

cloison de distribution *f* dividing wall

closoir de faîtage et de arêtier *m* roof ridge hip rafter flaunching

clôture *f* enclosure

clôture de bornage *f* boundary fence

clôture en béton *f* concrete fence

coffrage *m* formwork

coffret de forets/mèches *m* set of drill bits

coin *m* log-splitting wedge

colle à carreau de plâtre *f* plaster block adhesive

colle hydro *f* waterproof adhesive

colle matériaux d'isolation *f* insulating materials adhesive

colle néoprène *f* neoprene adhesive

collet *m* flange

colombage *m* half-timbering (typical of Normandy)

colonne *f* pillar

colorant *m* colourant

colorant béton et mortier *m* concrete and mortar colourant

colorant en poudre *m* powder colourant

colorant oxyde de fer *m* iron oxide colourant

combiner *v* to combine, to mix together *(see also: mêler)*

comble extérieur *m* eaves *(see also: avant-toit extérieur)*

combles perdus *mpl* eaves crawlspace

compacter *v* to compact

compresseur d'air *m* air compressor

compteur *m* electricity/water meter; counter

concasser *v* to crush

conduit de cheminée *m* chimney flue

conduit de cheminée en aluminium *m* aluminium chimney flue

conduit de cheminée en inox *m* stainless steel chimney flue

conduit de fumée en terre cuite *m* terracotta block chimney

conduit de cheminée isolé *m* insulated chimney flue

conduite *f* duct

contenance *f* capacity (e.g. of reservoir)

contrefiche *f* brace (of truss)

contre-fil *adj* against the grain (wood)

construire *v* to build *(see also: bâtir)*

contrat *m* contract

contremarche *f* staircase riser

convertir en *v* to convert into

cordeau de maçon *m* builder's string

corniche *f* cove; coving

cornière *f* angle iron

couche *f* layer

couche d'air *f* air gap (cavity wall)

couche de finition *f* finishing coat (e.g. plaster)

couche isolant *f* damp-proof course

coude *m* bend

coupe-boulons *m* bolt cutters

couper *v* to cut

cour *f* courtyard

cour anglaise *f* ventilation grille

cour intérieure *f* inner courtyard

couteau (*pl* **-x) à enduire** *m* caulker -s

couteau à joint pour plaques d'isolation *m* taping knife

couvercle *m* cover (e.g. inspection chamber)

couvrir *v* to cover

craie *f* chalk *(see also: poudre à tracer)*

crampillon *m* staple (hammer-in)

cramponner *v* to clamp

crémaillère *f* staircase string, open

crépi *m* rendering

crépir *v* to roughcast

crépissage *m* rendering; roughcasting

creuser *v* to dig

crochet ardoise *m* slate fixing hook

cuvette rotule *f* ball-socket

dallage *m* paving *(see also: pavage)*

dalle *f* paving stone

dalle de plafond *f* ceiling tile

dalle isolante/phonique *f* thermal sound insulating tile

dalle liège mur spécial isolation phonique *f* sound insulating cork wall tile

décapeur thermique *m* hot-air gun

déchet *m* refuse

décintroir à pic *m*; **~ double panne** *m* small, hand-held pick (not available in UK)

décoffrage décoffre *m* shuttering release agent

décoffrant démoulage *m* concrete mould release agent

décombres *mpl* debris

défaut *m* defect

défonceuse *f* router

déformation *f* warping

se déformer *v* to warp

dégagement *m* exit

délai *m* deadline; delay

délai de livraison *m* delivery date

délai de réflexion *m* cooling-off period

demi-brique *f* half-brick

démolir *v* to demolish

densité *f* density

déposer *v* to dump

déroulement *m* development (progress)

dessin *m* design; drawing

dessiner *v* to draw

devis *m* estimate

dévoiement *m* bend

diamètre *m* diameter

dilater *v* to expand

disque diamant *m* diamond cutting disc

dommage-ouvrage *m* construction fault/damage

dormant *m* window frame

doublage *m* lining

double vitrage *f* double glazing

drain agricole *m* land drainpipe

drainage *m* drainage

durcisseur de surface fixateur *m* concrete surface hardener

eau de la ville *f* mains water supply

éboulement *m* caving in

échafaudage *m* scaffolding

écharpe *f* brace (timber frame)

échelle *f* ladder

éclisse cornière *f* angle bead

écran de sous-toiture *m* roof underfelt

édifice *m* edifice

effrondrement *m* caving in

égoutter *v* to drain *(see also: vider)*

élévation *f* elevation

embase d'étanchéité cheminée *f* preformed chimney flaunching

emboîtement *m* housing boxing

en biseau *adj* bevelled

encorbellement *m* cantilever

enduire *v* to render

enduit *m* coating (e.g. plaster); filler; rendering

enduit à joint *m* jointing filler

enduit à joint prêt à l'emploi *m* ready to use filler

enduit à joint prise lente *m* slow-drying filler

enduit à prise rapide *m* quick-setting filler

enduit d'étanchéité *m* waterproof filler

enduit de finition *m* finishing filler

enduit de lissage *m* fine-surface filler

enduit de rebouchage *m* repair filler

enduit étance *m* sealant

enduit poudre à prise rapide *m* quick-setting jointing filler

enduit poudre de collage et finition *m* fine joint filler

enduit prêt à l'emploi *m* pre-mixed filler

enduit surfin *m* high quality filler

entraîneur d'air *m* concrete air entraining agent

entrée *f* entry; entrance

entrepreneur *m* contractor

entretoise *f* brace

équerre du maçon *f* builder's square

équipements *mpl* facilities

équiper *v* to fit

escabeau *f* stepladder

escalier *m* staircase

escalier deux quarts tournants *m* staircase with two quarter turns

escalier droit *m* straight staircase

escalier quart tournant bas *m* staircase, quarter turn at base

escalier quart tournant haut *m* staircase, quarter turn at top

escalier quart tournant milieu *m* staircase, quarter turn at centre

escalier quart tournant milieu avec palier *m* staircase, quarter turn at centre, with landing

escalier spirale *m*; ~ **en colimaçon** *m*; ~ **tournant** *m*; ~ **à vis**; ~ **à vis hélicoïdal carré** *m* spiral staircase

établi *m* workbench

étai *m* support prop

étai réglable *m* adjustable support

étanche *adj* waterproof; watertight; impermeable

étanchéité *f* waterproofing

étanchéité, bande de *f* flashing strip

étanchéité, bande de, indéchirable autocollante *f* non-tearing, self-adhesive flashing strip

étancher *v* to waterproof

éviter *v* to avoid

extérieur *m* exterior

extracteur éolien *m* chimney flue extractor

faîtage *m* roof ridge

fausse équerre *f* adjustable/sliding/combination bevel

faux limon *m* wall staircase string

faux plafond *f* false ceiling

fenêtre *f* window

fenêtre à battants *f* casement window

fenêtre à guillotine *f* sash window

fenêtre de toit *f* roof window

fer à joint plat *m* brick jointer

fer d'angle *m* angle iron

ferraillage *m* ironwork

ferme de charpente *f* truss *(see also: armature à toit)*

fermette *f* false gable; dormer window truss

fibres de verre *f* glass fibre

film à bulle d'air sec *m* air bubble layer (aluminium insulator)

fil à plomb maçon *m* plumbline

film armé réflecteur résistant à la déchirure *m* tear-resistant reflective membrane insulation

film extérieur réflecteur alu *m* outer aluminium film layer insulation

film réflecteur intermédiare *m* intermediate film layer insulation

fissure *f* crack

fixateur *m* setting agent

flocons de laine de roche en vrac *m* rockwool flakes in bulk

fondation *f* base

fondations *fpl* foundations

forer *v* to drill (a hole)

foret *m* drill bit *(see also: mèche)*

foret à béton *m* masonry drill bit

foret à métaux *m* metal drill bit

forets/mèches, coffret de set of drill bits

fossé *m* trench

fossé collecteur *m* drainage ditch

fosse d'aisance *f* cesspool

fossoyer *v* to dig a trench

foyer *m* hearth

fuseau *(pl -x)* *m* banister spindle -s

gâche *f* plaster mixing trowel

gâcher *v* to botch

gargouille *f* waterspout (guttering)

gaz *m* gas

gorge anti-refoulante *f* anti-backflow throat (fireplace)

gouttière *f* gutter

granulat *m* ballast

granulé isolant vermiculite *f* granulated vermiculite

gravier *m*; **gravillon** *m* gravel

gravillon roulé *m* rolled gravel

gravillon en vrac *m* bulk quantity gravel

grenier *m* loft

grès *m* sandstone

grille *f* bars (window); grille (e.g. inspection chamber)

grille caillebotis en acier galvanisé *f* galvanised metal grating

grille d'aeration *f* air grille

gros oeuvre *m* basic structure

groupe électrogène *m* generator

gypse *m* gypsum

gypse renforcé fibre *m* fibre reinforced gypsum

hache *f* axe

hachette *f* hatchet

hachette de plâtrier *f* lath/drywall hammer

hérissoner *v* to roughcast

hydrofuge liquide *m* liquid waterproofer

ignifuge *adj* fire-proof

imperméabilisant -e *adj* waterproofing

imperméable *adj* damp-proof

imprégnation incolore pour pavés et dalles béton *f* colourless waterproofing treatment for bases

ingénieur *m* engineer

insert de cheminée *m* fireplace insert

isolant *m* insulating material

isolant mince alu réfléchissant *m* aliminium foil reflective insulator

isolation film à bulle d'air sec *m* aluminium insulation air bubble layer

isolation film armé réflecteurs résistants à la déchirure *m* tear-resistant reflective insulation membrane

isolation film extériour réflecteur alu *m* exterior aluminium film layer

isolation film réflecteur intermédiaire *m* intermediate film layer (insulation)

isolation phonique *f*; ~ **acoustique** *f* soundproofing; sound insulation

isolation phonique pour sol humide *f* damp floors sound insulation

isolation phonique sols *f* soundproof membrane (floors)

isolation thermique *f* thermal/heat insulation

jumelé -e *adj* semi-detached

kit de débouchage *m* drain clearing kit

kit d'isolation de menuiseries *m* insulation kit (woodwork)

kit d'isolation pour porte de garage *m* insulation kit (garage door)

laine de chanvre *f* hemp wool

laine de roche *f* rockwool

laine de verre *f* glass wool

lambourde *f* floor batten

lambris *m* cladding; panelling; wainscoting

lambrissage *m* wainscoting

lambrisser *v* to wainscot

lame *f* blade

lame de scie *f* saw blade

largeur *m* breadth

latte *f* lath *(see also: volige)*

levier *m* lever

lézarde *f* crevice

liant *m* binding material

lier *v* to bind

lime *f* file

lime électrique *f* electric filer

limon *m* staircase string

limon, faux *m* staircase wall string

linteau *(pl -x)* *m* lintel -s

liquide incolore à base de resins *m* treatment, bases, resin (to protect and reinforce concrete slab)

lit de béton *m* bed of concrete

liteau *m* batten

liteau couverture *m* roof tiling batten

logement *m* apartment

longeron de faîtage *m* ridge bar

lucarne *f* dormer window

machine à crépir (tyrolienne) *f* spraying machine (Tyrolean)

maçonner *v* to brick; to brick up

madrier *m* large wooden beam

main-d'œuvre *f* labour

mairie *f* council offices

maison *f* house

malaxeur portif *m* mixing attachment

marbre *m* marble

marche *f* staircase tread

marteau (*pl* -x) *m* hammer -s

marteau à boucharder *m* sculptor's hammer (for dressing concrete, marble, granite)

marteau à briques *m* brick hammer

marteau arrache-clou *m* claw hammer

marteau de coffreur *m* packer's hammer (claw hammer)

marteau d'emballeur *m* packer's hammer

marteau démolisseur *m*; ~ **piqueur** *m* demolition drill

marteau perforateur *m* hammer drill (with or without cord)

martelette *f* small hammer (esp. slater's)

masse couple *f* sledgehammer

massette *f*; **marteau de maçon** *m* club/lump hammer

massif de fondation *m* foundation block

mastic *m* putty

mastic isolation portes-fenêtres *m* insulating mastic (doors and windows)

matériaux de revêtement *m* lining material

mèche *f* drill bit (*see also: foret*)

mèche à bois *f* wood drill bit

mèche à bois extensible *f* expansive drill bit

mèche à bois plate *f* flat drill bit

mèche à ogive/carbure/de tungstène *f* glass/ceramic/porcelain drill bit

mèche à spiral unique *f* auger bit

mèche hélicoidale *f* twist drill bit

mélange béton *m* concrete mix

mélanger *v* to mix (e.g. concrete)

mêler *v* to combine, to mix together (*see also: combiner*)

meneau (*pl* -x) *m* mullion -s

menuisier *m* joiner

merlin *m* poleaxe

mesure *f* measure

mesure pliante *f* folding rule

mesure roulante *f* retractable tape measure

mètre *m* metre

métré *m* estimate (quantities/costs)

mètre en cube *m* cubic metre

meuleuse d'angle *f* angle grinder

mignonnette non roulée *f* fine non-rolled gravel

moellon *m* building stone

montant métallique *m* reinforcement (partition framework)

mortier *m* mortar; grout

mortier à prise rapide *m* quick-setting mortar

mortier bâtard *m* lime mortar

mortier blanc *m* white mortar

mortier coloré *m* coloured mortar; ~ **beige foncé** *m* (dark beige); ~ **gris profond** *m* (dark grey); ~ **rose ambre** *m* (pink amber); ~ **rouge brique** *m* (brick red)

mortier d'imperméabilisation *m* waterproofing mortar

mortier de jointoiement *m* pointing mortar

mortier de ragréage et de lissage *m* finishing and smoothing mortar

mortier de réparation *m* repair mortar

mortier de réparation gris *m* grey repair mortar

mortier fin *m* fine mortar

mortier fin blanc *m* fine white mortar

mortier gris *m* grey mortar

mortier prêt à l'emploi *m* dry-mixed mortar

mortier prêt mix jointoiement gris *m* grey ready-mixed pointing mortar

mortier rapide *m* quick-setting mortar

mortier réfractaire *m* heat-resistant/refractory mortar

mortier réparation kit *m* restoration mortar kit for concrete

mousse expansée *f* foam rubber

mousse expansive polyuréthane *f* expanding polyurethane foam filler

mulot *m* half-width brick

mur *m* wall

mur mitoyen *m* party wall

mur portant *m* load-bearing wall

murer *v* to brick; to wall

muret béton décoratif *m* decorative concrete walling block

muret pierre reconstituée *m* reconstituted stone walling block

nettoyeur haute pression *m* high pressure cleaner

niveau (*pl* -x) *m* level -s

niveau à bulle *m* spirit level

niveau laser *m* laser level

noyau d'escalier *m* staircase newel post

obstruction *f* blockage

oriel *m* bay/bow window

orifice *m* aperture

orifice de ramonage *m* access aperture for cleaning (e.g. soot box)

ossature métallique *f* metal frame (partition wall)

outillage électroportatif *m* portable power tools

outillage électroportatif, accessoires *m* power tool accessories

ouverture *f* hole

palier *m* staircase landing

panne *f* purlin

panne faîtière *f* ridge purlin

panne sablière *f* eaves purlin

panneau *m* fascia; panel

panneau de cheminée *m* chimney panel

panneau de doublage plaque de plâtre *m* plasterboard with central insulating layer

panneau de particules *m* chipboard

panneau laine de roche *m* rockwool panel

panneau laine de roche non revêtue *m* unsurfaced rockwool panel

pare-vapeur, ~ kraft *m* damp-proof membrane

paroi *f* face (e.g. of a wall)

paroi verticale *f* vertical partition

parpaing *m* breezeblock

passe plat *m* serving hatch

pâte *f* putty

pavage *m* paving *(see also: dallage)*

pavé *m* flagstone; cobblestone

pavé -e *adj* paved

pavé -e de brique *adj* brick-paved

pelle *f* shovel; spade

pelle carrée *f* square shovel

pelle ronde *f* round shovel

percer *v* to drill (a hole in a board)

perceuse *f* drill

perceuse à percussion filaire *f* corded percussion drill

perceuse à percussion sans fil *f* cordless percussion drill

perceuse visseuse *f* drill/screwdriver

perforateur électropneumatique *m* pneumatic hammer drill

permis de construire *m* building permit

pièce *f* room

pied-de-biche *m* crowbar

pierre *f* stone

pierre calcaire *f* limestone

pigment naturel *m* natural pigment; ~ **ocre jaune** *m* (yellow ochre); ~ **terre d'ombre** *m* (umber); ~ **terre de sienne** *m* (sienna)

pignon *m* gable

pilier *m* walling block pillar

pince à décoffrer *f* wrecking bar

pioche *f* pick

pioche de cantonnier *f* mattock

pioche hache; ~ **de terrassier** *f* pick axe

placard *m* built-in cupboard

plafond *m* ceiling

planche *f* floorboard

planche d'échafaudage *f* scaffold board

planche de rive *f* gutter board

planchéiage *m* boarding

plancher *m* floor; flooring

plancher précontraint *m* prestressed flooring beam

plan *m* drawing

planelle *f* thin profile breezeblock (not available in UK)

planelle perforée *f* thin profile hollow breezeblock (not available in UK)

plaque d'égout *f* manhole cover

plaque de gypse *f* gypsum board

plaque de plâtre *f* plasterboard

plaque de plâtre de sol *f* flooring plasterboard

plaque de plâtre feu *f* firecheck plasterboard

plaque de plâtre haute densité *f* high density plasterboard

plaque de plâtre ignifugée *f*
fireproofed plasterboard

**plaque isolante et
réfléchissante** *f* radiator
reflector

plaque ondulée *f* corrugated
roof panel

plaquette *f* wall tile

plaquette de parement *f* facing
brick (or facing block)

plastifiant *m* plasticiser

plâtre *m* plaster

plâtre à modeler *m* moulding
plaster

plâtre à projecter *m*
projection plaster

plâtre allégé *m* alleviated
plaster

plâtre de Paris *m* plaster of
Paris

plâtre en poudre *m* powder
plaster

plâtre fin blanc *m* fine white
plaster

plâtre incendie *m* fire-
resistant plaster

plâtre manuel *m* hand-
mixing plaster

plâtre manuel gros *m*
backing plaster

plâtre multi-usage *m* multi-
finish plaster; universal plaster

plâtre ponce *m* pumice plaster

plâtre prestia *m* casting plaster

plâtrer *v* to plaster

platroir à enduire *m* cement
trowel; finishing trowel; flooring
trowel; plasterer's trowel

platroir à enduire denté *m*
notched trowel

platroir à enduire inoxidable
m steel float

platroir inoxidable *m* steel
float

plinthe *f* skirting board; base-
board

poignée pare-coup *f* protective
hand grip for chisel

pointerolle de maçon *f*
masonry chisel; (nearest
equivalent) plugging chisel

polystyrène adjuvanté *m*
polystyrene aggregate

polystyrène expansé *m*
expanded polystyrene

polystyrène extrudé *m*
extruded polystyrene

**polystyrène extrudé bord
droit** *m* square-edged extruded
polystyrene board

polystyrène extrudé bord rainuré *m* groove-edged extruded polystyrene board

polyuréthane *m* polyurethane

ponceuse *f* sander

ponceuse à bande *f* belt sander

ponceuse delta *f* delta sander

ponceuse excentrique *f* disc sander

ponceuse vibrantes *f* orbital sander

porche *m* porch

porte *f* gate

porte de derrière *f* back door

porte-fenêtre *f* French window

porte-outils *m* toolbox

pose *f* placing; installing

pose-dalle *f* slab lifter

poser *v* to lay

poudre *f* powder

poudre à tracer *f* chalk *(see also: craie)*

pourriture sèche *f* dry rot

poussière *f* dust

poutre *f*; **poutrelle** *f* beam

poutre apparente *f* exposed beam

poutre de rive *f* edge beam (e.g. wall plate)

poutre en fer *f* girder; RSJ (rolled steel joist)

poutre précontrainte *f*; **poutrelle céramique** *f*; **poutrelle béton** *f* prestressed concrete beam

préfabrication *f* prefabrication

prelinteau précontraint *m* prestressed concrete lintel

premier étage *m* first floor

prise d'air *f* air inlet

produit de cure *m* concrete cure

profondeur *m* depth

protection soubassement *f* damp-proof membrane

protège angle galvanisé *m* galvanised aluminium plaster bead

quincaillerie *f* hardware

rabot *m* plane

raccordement aux égouts *m* connecting to the drains

ragréer *v* to clean down (brickwork)

raidisseur *m* brace

rail métallique *m* metal rail (partition wall)

rainure *f* groove

rainurer *v* to groove

rainureuse *f* wall chaser attachment

rampe *f* banister (handrail)

rampe d'éscalier *f* flight of stairs

ravalement *m* resurfacing

rebord de fenêtre *m* window sill

reboucher *v* to block up; to fill a crack

refaire la surface *v* to resurface

regard *m* inspection chamber; manhole

regard béton (avec couvercle ou grille) *m* concrete inspection chamber (with cover or grille)

regard d'assainissement *m* manhole

regard de branchement pour eaux pluviales *m* rainwater gully

regard de drainage *m* manhole

règle de maçon *f* rule (darby)

réglementation *f* control

rejointoiement *m* repointing

remblayer *v* to fill

remettre à neuf *v* refurbish

rénovation *f* renovation

rénover *v*; **restaurer** *v* to renovate

réparation béton *f* concrete repairer/restorer

réservoir bassin *m* fishpond

réservoir d'eau *m* cistern

résine à base de latex *f* latex-based resin

résine d'adjonction *f* resin binder

résistance au feu *f* fire resistance

retardateur de prise pour béton *m* concrete set retarder

rétrécissement *m* contraction

revêtement *m* cladding; lining

revêtement bitumineux *m* bituminous liquid

revêtement d'imperméabilisation pour travaux de cuvelages *m* waterproofing treatment for cellars

revêtement imperméable *m* waterproof coating

rez-de-chaussée *m* ground floor

rigole *f* foundation trench

rive de tête *f* top side of a hipped roof

rive de toit *f* roof verge

rive latérale *f* side of a hipped roof

rouleau *m* roll

rouleau de laine de verre *m* glass wool roll

rouleau multi-réflecteur *m* refective roof insulation roll

sable *m* sand

sable à maçonner *m* masonry sand

sable argenté *m* silver sand

sable de mélange béton *m* concreting sand

sable doux *m* soft sand

sable en vrac *m* bulk quantity sand

sable liant *m*; ~ **mordant** *m* sharp sand

sable de rivière *m* river sand

sableuse *f* sandblaster

sabot de poutre *f* joist hanger

sac de ciment *m* sack of cement

sans amiante *adj* asbestos free

sceller *v* to seal

scie *f* saw

scie à métaux *f* hacksaw

scie circulaire *f* circular saw

scie-cloche *f* hole saw

scie sabre *f* sabre saw

scie sauteuse *f* jig saw

scie tronçonneuse *f* chain saw

seau (*pl* -x) de maçon *m* builder's bucket

serre-joint de cimentier *m* formwork clamp

serre-joint de maçon *m* mason's clamp

serrer *v* to clamp

sol *m* floor; ground

solin *m* coating of fill-in material (e.g. plaster, mortar)

solive *f* joist

sortie de toit *f* prefabricated chimney stack

sous-sol *m* basement

sous-couche liège isol carrelage *f* cork insulating underlay (tiles)

sous-couche liège isol moquette *f* cork insulating underlay (fitted carpet)

sous-couche liège sol isolation phonique *f* cork soundproofing underlay (floors)

support *m* bearer

surbaisser *v* to lower

suspente pour laine de verre *f* insulation suspension clip

taloche *f* plasterer's float; hawk *(see also: platroir)*

taloche bois *f* wooden float

taloche plastique *f* plastic float

taloche polystyrène *f* foam float

tamis *m* sieve

télémètre laser *m* laser measure

terrain constructible *m* building land

terrasse *f* patio

terre *f* ground

tirer des plans *v* to draw plans

toile de jute *f* hessian

toit *m* roof

toit-terrasse *m* flat roof

tout a l'égout *m* mains sewer

tracer *v* to draw

traitement caves et sous-sols *m* treatment for cellars

traitement façades murs extérieurs *m* exterior masonry treatment

traitement imprégnation incolore pour pavés et dalles béton *m* colourless waterproofing for paving and concrete slabs

traitement incolore antimousse *m* colourless anti-moss masonry treatment

traitement incolore d'imperméabilisant *m* colourless water repellent masonry treatment

traitement liquide incolore à base de resines *m* colourless resin (to protect and reinforce concrete slab)

traitement revêtement d'imperméabilisation pour travaux de cuvelages *m* waterproofing treatment for cellars

traitement sols *m* treatment for bases

tranchée *f* trench

travailleur *m* labourer

traverse *f* transom; cross-bar

treillis *m* trellis

trémie *f* cavity

trémie de cheminée *f* chimney opening

tréteau *m* trestle

triangle de laine de roche *m* rockwool triangle

tronçonneuse *f* chain saw

trou *m* hole

trappe de visite *m* manhole

truelle *f* trowel; ~ **à brique** *f* (bricklaying); ~ **ronde** *f* (rounded tip); ~ **italienne** *f* (pointed tip)

truelle carrée *f* bucket trowel (square edged)

truelle d'angle *f* corner trowel

truelle langue de chat *f* pointing trowel (English:

pointed tip; French: rounded
tip); (nearest equivalent)
gauging trowel

truelle triangulaire *f* no
equivalent in UK

trumeau *m* arch pillar;
overmantel

tubage de conduit flexible *m*
flexible chimney flue liner

tube d'assainissement *m*; **tube
de drainage** *m* drainpipe

tuile *f* roofing tile

tuile à chatière grillagée *f*
ventilator tile *(see also: tuile à
douille)*

tuile à côtes *f* interlocking
ribbed tile

tuile à douille *f* ventilator tile
(see also: tuile à chatière grillagée)

tuile à onde douce *f*
interlocking shallow curved
tile; **~ à emboîtement
grande moule faiblement
galbée** *f* (large mould, shallow
curve); **~ à emboîtement
petit moule faiblement
galbée** *f* (small mould, shallow
curve)

tuile canal *f* pantile; roman tile

tuile creuse *f* gutter tile

tuile de rive *f* verge tile

tuile en verre transparente *f*
transparent tile

tuile faîtière *f* ridge tile

tuile plate *f* plain tile

tuile plate à emboîtement
f; **~ plate à emboîtement
à pureau plat** *f* interlocking
flat tile

tuile romaine *f* half-round tile

**tuile romaine, grande
moule fortement galbée** *f*
interlocking roman tile (large
mould, deep curve)

tuyau de descente *m* downpipe
(guttering)

ventilateur *m* fan

ventilateur électrique *m*
electric fan

ventilateur extracteur *m*
extractor fan

ventouse *f* air vent (of fireplace)

vermiculite *f* vermiculite

**vermiculite enrobée de
bitume** *f* bitumen-coated
vermiculite

verrière *f* glass roof

vidanger *v* to empty out

vide *m* empty space

vide *adj* empty

vider *v* to clear; to drain; to
   empty *(see also: égoutter)*
visseuse *f* screwdriver (with or
   without cord)
**voile protecteur en
   polypropylène** *f* protective
   polypropylene layer
volige *f* lath *(see also: latte)*
voûte *f* arch

NOTES

CHARPENTERIE

CARPENTRY

about *m* butt

abouter *v* to butt

acajou *m* mahogany

affûtage *m* grinding

affûter *v* to grind

affûteuse *f* grinder

agrafe *f* staple

alaise rapportée *f* door edging

arbre *m* tree

arrondi -e *adj* rounded

assemblage *m* assembly; assembling

assemblage à demis-bois *m* cross-halving joint

assemblage à mi-bois *m* halving joint

assemblage à tenon et mortaise *m* mortise and tenon joint

assemblage queue d'aronde *m* dovetail joint

assembler *v* to assemble

astragale *m* astragal moulding

avant-toit *m* eaves

avivé -e *adj* sharpened/square cut

baguette *f* beading/casing

baguette d'angle *f* right-angle moulding

balustre *m* banister

banc *m* lathe bed

bastaing *m* plank (10" x 2 ½")

bédane de menuisier *m* mortise chisel; bedane (chisel for woodturning)

biseau (*pl* -x) *m* bevel *(see also: chanfrein)*

biseauter *v* to bevel *(see also: chanfreiner)*

bloc *m* block

bloc-moteur *m* lathe motor block

bois *m* wood

bois brut *m* untreated wood

bois de charpente *m* timber

bois de couverture *m* roofing wood

bois dur *m* hardwood

bois raboté *m* planed wood

bois tendre *m* softwood

boisage *m* timberwork

boiser *v* to wainscot

boiserie *f* woodwork

boîte à onglets *f* mitre box

boulon *m* bolt

bouton de porte *m* door knob

broche *f* lathe spindle

brossé -e *adj* brushed

cadre *m* frame

cale *f* wedge; sandpaper block

caler *v* to wedge

calibre *m* bore

chambranle *m* window frame moulding

chanfrein *m* bevel; bevelled edge; chamfer

chanfreiner *v* to chamfer

chant plat *m* flat edge moulding

charnière *f* hinge

charpente *f* structure/ framework **charpente en bois** *f* timber frame

charpentier *m* carpenter

chasse-clou *m* nail punch

chêne *m* oak

cheville *f* dowel; pin *(see also: tourillon)*

chevron *m* rafter/chevron

chevronnage *m* raftering

chignole *f* hand drill

cimaise *f* picture frame moulding

cintre *m* arch

ciré -e *adj* polished

ciseau (*pl* -x) à bois *m* wood chisel -s

ciseau à grain d'orge *m* parting chisel (woodturning)

ciseau à racler arrondis *m* scraper (woodturning)

ciseau de charpentier *m* firmer chisel

ciseau de menuisier *m*; **ciseau de sculpteur** *m* bevel-edged chisel

ciseau droit *m* straight chisel (woodturning)

ciseler *v* to chisel

clou *m* nail *(see also: pointe)*

clou à bateaux *m* flooring nail

clou à beton *m* masonry nail

clou à tête diamant *m* clout nail

clou à tête d'homme *m* oval wire nail

clou à tête perdue *m*; **~ étêté** *m*; **~ sans tête** *m* brad

clou à tête plate *m* round wire nail

clou à tête plate, 'extra large' *m* extra large head clout nail

clou de Paris *m* wire nail

clou de vitrier *m* glazing sprig

clou découpé *m*; **clou étampé** *m* cut nail

clou doré *m* brass-headed nail

clou ondulé *m* corrugated fastener

clou sans tête *m* lost head nail *(see also: clou à tête perdue)*

clou torsadé *m* twisted shank nail

clouer *v* to nail

coffrage *m* boxing; framework; shuttering

coller *v* to glue

colombage *m* half-timbered

compas d'épaisseur *m* caliper gauge (woodturning)

contre-plaqué *m*; **contre-collé** *m* plywood

copieur universel *m* lathe copy turning attachment

corniche *f* cornice moulding

couteau *m* knife

coutellerie *f* knives

couvre-chant *m*; **alaise rapportée** *f* door edging

couvre-joint *m* cover strip moulding

couvre-joint carrelage *m* cover strip moulding for tiles

couvre-joint cloison *m* cover strip moulding for walls

crayon charpente *m* carpenter's pencil

crochet à lambris *m*; **clip à frisette** *m* metal clip for T&G panelling

déformation *f* buckling; warping

dessiner *v* to draw

dimensions *fpl* dimensions

dosse *f* flitch of timber (slab, cut lengthways from a tree trunk)

éclat *m* splinter

emboîtement *m* interlocking; fitting

encadrement *m* framing moulding

en kit *m* flat pack

entaillage *m* notching

entaille *f* notch

entailler *v* to notch

épaisseur *f* thickness

épicéa *m* spruce

équerre *f* try square

établi de bois *m* carpenter's bench

établi-étau *m*; ~ **pliante et réglable** *m* portable workbench-vice

étagère *f* shelf

étau *m* vice

éventail *m* lathe tool rest

façade cantonnière *f* façade/frontage pelmet

fausse équerre *f* adjustable/sliding/combination bevel

fausse languette *f* false tongue (joint)

fente *f* cleft

fibre de bois *f* wood grain

fil de bois *m* grain (of wood)

finition *f* finish; finishing

foret *m* drill bit; twist drill bit

foret expansif *m* expansive drill bit

foret vrille *m* auger drill bit

frêne *f* ash

frise *f* border; frieze

frise décorative *f* decorative border

gerce *f* cleft

gond *m* hinge

gouge *f* gouge (woodturning)

gouge à creuser *f* bowl gouge

gouge à dégrossir *f* roughing-out gouge

gouge à profiler *f* spindle gouge

gouge bouteille *f* bottle gouge

gouge conique *f* conical gouge

grand serre-joint *m* sash clamp

hache *f* axe

hachette de charpentier *f* carpenter's hammer

herminette *f* adze

hêtre *m* beech

huile *f* oil

huile de lin *f* linseed oil

huiler *v* to oil

huisserie *f* door frame

iroko *m* iroko

isorel *m*; **fibres dures** *fpl* hardboard

jalonner *v* to mark out

joint bout à bout *m* butt joint

lambris *m* panelling; wainscoting

lambrissage *m* wainscoting

lambrisser *v* to wainscot

lame *f* strip of wood; blade

laque *f* shellac

laqué -e *adj* lacquered

laquer *v* to lacquer; to shellac

largeur *f* width

latte *f* lath

latté *m* blockboard

lime *f* file

lisse *adj* smooth

lisser *v* to smooth

liteau *m* roofing batten

longueur *f* length

madrier *m* large beam

maillet *m* mallet

maillet d'ébéniste *m* cabinet maker's mallet (round head)

maillet de menuisier *m* woodwork mallet (square head)

main courante *f* banister rail

marteau (*pl* -x) *m* hammer -s

marteau à menuisier *m* carpenter's hammer

marteau arache-clou *m*; ~ **de coffreur** *m* claw hammer

marteau d'emballeur *m* packer's hammer

massif -ive *adj* solid

mastic pâte à bois *m* woodfiller

MDF *m* MDF (medium density fibreboard)

mèche plate *f* flat/spade drill bit

mesurer *v* to measure

mètre pliant *m* folding rule

mortaise *f* mortise

moulure *f* moulding

moulure demi-rond *f* half-round moulding

nez de marche *m* rounded lip moulding for stairs

niangon *m* niangon

noeud *m* knot

noyer *m* walnut

orme *m* elm

palissade *f* fencing

palissandre *m* rosewood

panne *f* purlin

panneau (*pl* **-x**) *m* panel -s

panneau d'aggloméré *m*; ~ **de particules** *m* chipboard

papier de verre *m* glasspaper; sandpaper

parfaire *v* to finish off

parquet *m* parquet flooring

parquet à coller *m* glued parquet

paumelle *f* door hinge

percer *v* to bore; drill

perceuse *f* drill

peuplier *m* poplar

pignon *m* gable

pin *m* pine

pince à ressort *f* spring clamp

pince de serrage *f* handy clamp

pince étau à cliquet *f* ratchet clamp

pin des Landes *m* pine from Landes region of France

pin maritime *m* maritime pine

pin massif *m* solid pine

piquet de clôture *m* fence post

placage *m* veneering

plafond *m* ceiling

planche *f* board; plank; flooring batten

planche à dresser *f* shooting board

planche bouvetée *f* matchboard

planche de rive *f* fascia board

planche mobile *f* loose board plank

planches de recouvrement *f* weatherboarding

plane *m* skew chisel (woodturning); drawknife

plateau de tournage *m* lathe faceplate

plinthe *f* skirting board

plinthe plaquée *f* veneered skirting board

pointe *f* nail; tack *(see also: clou)*

pointe à ardoise *f* slate peg

pointe décorative à tête bombée *f* dome-headed upholstery pin

pointe *f*; **petit clou** *m*; **clou de bouche** *m*; **clou de soufflet** *m* tack

poncer *v* to sand; to sand down; to sandpaper

ponceuse *f* sander

ponceuse à bande *f* belt sander

ponceuse delta *f* delta sander

ponceuse excentrique *f* disc sander

ponceuse vibrantes *f* orbital sander

portail en bois *m* wooden gate -s

porte *f* door; gate

poupée fixe *f* lathe headstock

poupée mobile *f* lathe tailstock

pourrir *v* to decay

pourrissement *m* decay

pourriture sèche *f* dry rot

poutre *f* beam; baulk

poutre apparentre *f* exposed beam

poutre maîtresse *f*; **poutre principale** *f* main beam

poutrelle *f* small beam

pré-encollé -e *adj* pre-glued

presse de mécanicien *f* G-clamp

quart-de-rond *m* (*pl* **quarts-de-rond**) quarter-round moulding

rabot *m* plane

rabot fonte *m* block plane

rabot guillaume *m* rebate plane

rabot manuel *m*; **~ semelle métal** *m* hand/jack plane

rabot métallique *m* smoothing plane

rabot moulure *m* moulding plane

rabot racloir acier *m* spokeshave *(see also: vastringue)*

rabot Surform *m* planer file (Surform)

raboter *v* to plane

racloir de finiton *m* scraper

ragréer *v* to finish off

rainé -e *adj* grooved

rainé -e en bout *adj* grooved end/tip

rainer *v* to groove

ramin *m* ramin

rampe d'escalier *f* banisters

râpe *f* rasp

refendre *v* to cleave; to split

refente *f* cleaving

règle *f* rule

réglet inox flexible *f* flexible steel rule

repère de tourillon *m* dowel pin

rifloir *m* rifler file

rosace de plafond *f* ceiling rose

sapin *m* fir

sapin blanc du nord *m* white fir (from the north of France)

scie *f* saw

scie à araser *f* gents/back saw

scie à chantonner *f* coping/fret saw

scie à dos *f* tenon saw

scie à guichet *f* pad saw

scie à main *f* handsaw

scie à métaux *f* hacksaw

scie à monture de menuisier *f* frame saw

scie à onglet *f* mitre saw

scie à panneaux *f* panel saw (for man-made boards and natural timber)

scie à placage *f* veneer saw

scie à ruban *f* band saw

scie de charpentier *f* carpenter's saw

scie égoïne coupe fine *f* hand saw for mouldings, panelling

scie égoïne grosse coupe *f*; ~ **à denture américaine** *f* hand saw for constructional timber such as rafters, formwork and planks

scie égoïne pour coupe longitudinal *f* rip saw for cutting along the grain

scie égoïne pour coupe transversal *f* cross-cut saw for cutting across the grain

scie égoïne universelle *f* all-purpose saw (for man-made boards and natural timber)

scie sauteuse *f* jigsaw

scier *v* to saw

semence de tapissier *f* upholstery tack

serre-jointe *m* clamp

serre-joint à pompe *m*; **presse mâchoire** *m* F-style gripper clamp

serre-joint automatique *m* bar clamp; speed clamp

solive *f* joist

soliveau (*pl* -x) *m* small joist

Surform; rabot Surform *m* Surform tool

tablette *f* shelf

tarière *f* gimlet

tarière à gouge *f* bradawl

tasseau (*pl* -x) *m* length of wood

teck *m* teak

teinté -e *adj* stained; tinted

tenon *m* tenon

tour à bois *m* lathe

tourillon *m* dowel *(see also: cheville)*

tracer *v* to draw

traverse *f* cross beam

tronçonneuse *f* chainsaw

trusquin *m*; **troussequin** *m* marking/mortise gauge

vastringue *f* spokeshave *(see also: rabot racloir acier)*

veinage de bois *m* wood veining

ver du bois *m* woodworm

vernir *v* to varnish

vernis *m* varnish

vernis clair *m* clear varnish

vernis mat *m* matt varnish

vernis satiné *m* satin varnish

vernissage *m* varnishing

vilebrequin *f* brace

vis à bois *f* woodscrew

vis à bois et aggloméré *f* chipboard woodscrew

vis à tête fendue *f* slot-headed woodscrew

vis empreinte cruciforme (Phillips) *f* cross-headed (Phillips) woodscrew

vis empreinte cruciforme (Posidriv) *f* cross-headed (Posidriv) woodscrew

vis empreinte cruciforme (TORX) *f* cross-headed (TORX) woodscrew

vis fraisée bombée *f* slot-headed round topped woodscrew

vis plaque de platre *f* plasterboard screw

vis plate, fraisée et fendue *f* slot-headed countersunk woodscrew

vis ronde fendue *f* domed slot-
headed woodscrew

vis spéciale indesserrable *f*
non-removable woodscrew

visser *v* to screw

volet *m* shutter

volige *f* thin plank

vrille *f* auger (for making pilot
holes)

wengé *m* wenge

NOTES

DECORATION

DECORATING

accélérateur de séchage *m*
paint-drying accelerator

acétone *f* acetone

ajouré -e *adj* hemstitched

anneau (*pl* **-x) à rideaux** *m* curtain
ring -s

antirouille *m* rust inhibitor

**antirouille primaire
protecteur** *m* metal primer

applique auto-collant *f* self-
adhesive tile transfer

apprêt *m* primer

arrêt de cordon *m;* **taquet** *m* cleat

assouplisseur *m* softener

avant-peinture *m* primer

bac spécial à réservoir *m* roller
tray *(see also: égouttoir)*

badigeon coloré à la chaux *m*
colourwashing

**badigeon effet douceur blanc
à colorer** *m* white colourwash
paint (for adding colorant)

bandes de couleur *fpl* masking

barre à rideaux *f;* **tringle
chemin de fer** *f* curtain
rail/rod

batte *f* float (for pressing down
tiles)

bec-de-perroquet *m* ceramic tile
nibblers

**boîte à coupe (moulures et
corniches de plafond)** *f*
mitre box (for cutting ceiling
mouldings and cornices)

brosse *f* brush; paintbrush *(see
also: pinceau)*

brosse à badigeon *f* whitewash/
emulsion paintbrush

brosse à décaper *f* rotary wire
brush (for power drill)

brosse à encoller *f* pasting brush

brosse à la main métallique *f*
hand-held wire brush

brosse à lessiver *f* cleaning/
washing brush

brosse à plafond *f* ceiling
paintbrush

brosse à pocher *f* stippling brush

brosse à raccords *f* touching up
paintbrush

brosse à rechampir *f* pointed
paintbrush (for delicate work)

brosse à tableaux plate *f* small
flat paintbrush (for touching
up and detailed/artistic
paintwork)

brosse à tableaux ronde *f* small
round paintbrush (for touching
up and detailed/artistic
paintwork)

brosse de pouce *f* round-stock paintbrush (rounded end to bristles)

brosse de tapissier *f* paperhanging brush

brosse douce *f* soft brush (paint effects)

brosse douce synthétique *f* synthetic soft brush (paint effects)

brosse en poils de blaireau *f* badger brush

brosse hermétique *f* paintbrush with tightly packed bristles

brosse plate à lacquer *f* flat lacquer brush

brosse plate extra-épaisse *f* extra thick brush

brosse pour effet moucheté *f* dragging brush (paint effect)

brosse radiateur coudée à plat *f* radiator paintbrush (forward-angled)

brosse radiateur coudée sur chant *f* radiator paintbrush (side-angled)

brosse rectangulaire *f* rectangular paintbrush

brosse ronde *f* whitewash/emulsion/paste paintbrush (round-stock, large, squared end to bristles)

brosser *v* to brush

cache noeud *f*; **gland noeud** *m* curtain cord pull; acorn

cadre *m* frame

cadre à poser *m* photograph frame

cale à poncer *f* sanding block

carreau *(pl* **-x)** *m* tile -s

carreau céramique *m* ceramic tile

carreau de sol en PVC *m* PVC tile

carreau liège *m* cork tile

carreau pierre reconstituée *m* reconstituted stone tile

carreau vinyle *m* vinyl tile

carrelage *m* tiling

chiffon *m* rag

ciment joint *m* tile cement

cire carrelage *f* tile wax/polish

cisailles *fpl* wirecutters

ciseaux *mpl* scissors

ciseaux de décoration *mpl* decorator's scissors

ciseaux gros travaux *mpl* heavy duty scissors

ciseaux multi-use/universel *mpl* multi-use scissors

colle *f* glue; paste

colle murale liège *f* cork glue

colle pour frise *f*; ~ **renforcée frise** *f* border/frieze glue

colle pour raccord *f*; ~ **renforcée raccord** *f* touch up glue (for wallpaper)

coller *v* to glue

collier d'angle *m* curtain corner bracket

coloris *m* colour; shade

concentré de pigments à effet nacré et coloré *m* pearl-coloured colouriser

copie au pochoir *m* stencilling *(see also: flocage)*

couche *f* coat (of paint etc.)

couche, première *f* base coat

coupe *f* cutter

coupe-carrelage *m* tile-cutters

coupe-carrelage électrique *m* electric tile-cutter

coupe-carrelage manuel *m* flat bed tile-cutter

coupe-verre *f* glass cutter

couteau *(pl* -x*) m* knife -ves

couteau à colle *m* adhesive comb knife

couteau à enduire *m* smoothing knife (for filler)

couteau à joint pour plaques d'isolation *m* scraping knife (for pointing insulation panels)

couteau de peintre *m* paint scraping knife

crépi *m* stucco (not generally available in UK)

crépir *v* to stucco

croisillon *m* tile spacer

cutter *m* craft knife

dalle *f* large floor tile; paving stone

dalle moquette *f* carpet tile

décapant carrelage spécial tâches de graisse *m* grease stain stripper (removal of grease stains from tiles)

décapant carrelage spécial tâches organiques *m* biological stain stripper (removal of biological stains from tiles)

décapant voile et laitance ciment carrelage non émaillé *m* stain stripper (removal of cement stains from un-glazed tiles)

décirant *f* polish/shine remover

décolleuse *f* steam stripper

décolleuse à vapeur *m* wallpaper steam stripper

décolleuse de papiers peints *f* chemical wallpaper stripper

décolleuse de peint *f* chemical paint stripper

décor *m* decor/decoration

décoratif -ive *adj* decorative

découper électrique de papier peint *m* electric wallpaper cutter

dégraissant *m* degreaser

détachant *m* stain remover

diluant *m* thinner

diluant cellulosique *m* cellulose paint thinner

diluant synthétique *m* synthetic paint thinner

disque diamant carrelage *f* diamond tile-cutting disc

dissolvant *m* solvent

durcisseur *m* hardener

durcisseur pour plâtre *m* stabilising primer

écaillé -e *adj* chipped/flaking

effet marbrant *m* marbling (paint effect)

effets de peinture *mpl* paint effects

égouttoir *m* roller tray (see also: bac spécial à réservoir)

époussette *m* dusting brush

encadre *v* to frame

encadrement *m* framing

encollage *m* gluing

encolleuse *m* ready-pasted wallpaper soaking tray

enduit *m* grout

éponge naturelle *f* natural sponge

éponge synthétique *f* synthetic sponge

équerre de serrage et cordeau de tension *f* corner frame clamp (with tensioning cord)

essuyage *m* ragging (paint effect)

etamine *f* muslin

faux-finis *f* faux finish (paint effect)

fibre de verre *m* glass fibre

fibre de verre anti-fissure *f* anti-crack glass fibre

fibre de verre mini-maille *f* fine mesh glass fibre

fibre de verre non-inflammable *f* non-inflammable glass fibre

fibre de verre prépeinte *f* prepainted glass fibre

flocage *m* stencilling (see also: copie au pochoir)

frottage *m* frotting/rubbed paint effect

frottis *m* scumble (paint effect)

gant à peindre en peau de mouton *m* lambswool painting mitt

gants de caoutchouc *mpl* rubber gloves

genouillère *f* tiler's knee pad

glacis *m* glaze

glacis à craqueler *m* crackle glaze

glacis à la cire *m* wax glaze

glacis à l'huile *m* oil glaze

glacis acrylique *m* acrylic glaze

glose *f* gloss

grattoir à fissures triangulaire *m* triangular shave hook

grattoir à lame *m* scratching blade

grille abrasive *f* abrasive mesh

huile de lin *f* linseed oil

imperméabilisant carreaux *adj* tile waterproofer

joint en pâte *m* tile joint sealant

jointoyer *v* to grout

kit barre à rideaux *m* curtain rail kit

laine d'acier *f* wire wool

lame d'arasement *f* wallpaper trimming wheel *(see also: roulette d'arasement)*

lame rétractable *f* retractable blade

laqué -e *adj* gloss

lasure *f* stain/tint

lessivable *adj* washable

lessive pour peinture *f* washing liquid for paint

liège *m* cork

lin *m* linen

malaxeur de peinture *m* paint mixer

manche *m* handle (of paintbrush)

manchon *m* roller sleeve

marqueterie *f* marquetry; inlaid work; mosaic

mastic *m* putty

mastique fixation cartouche *m* joint mastic (in tube)

mat -e *adj* matt

mélangeur *m* mixer

métallisé -e *adj* metallic finish

mini rouleau *m* mini roller

monture *f* roller frame

moquette *f* carpet; carpeting

moquette à relief *f* raised pile carpet

moquette berbère *f* Berber carpet

moquette bouclée *f* looped carpet

moquette fibres de coco *f*
cocoa fibre carpet

moquette imprimée *f* printed
carpet

moquette laine *f* wool carpet

moquette tressée *f* woven
carpet

moquette velours *f* velvet pile
carpet

moulure decorative *f*
decorative moulding

mur masqué *m* masked wall

ne jaunit pas *expr* non-
yellowing

nettoyant carreaux *m* tile
cleaner

nettoyant outils peinture *m*
brush/painting equipment
cleaner

nettoyeur pour store vénitien
m venetian blind cleaner

nuancier chromatique *m*
colour chart

œillet *m* eyelet

outil à veiner effet bois *m*
wood graining effect tool

palette à peindre *m* paint palette

papier abrasif *m* abrasive paper

papier de verre *m* sandpaper

papier peint *m* wallpaper

papier peint à peindre *m*
wallpaper for painting

papier peint à peindre motif
naturel (incrustation de
copeaux de bois) *m* woodchip
wallpaper

papier peint effet pommelé
m dappled effect wallpaper (for
painting)

papier peint effet tissé *m*
woven effect wallpaper

papier peint gaufré *m*
embossed wallpaper

papier peint lavable *m*
washable wallpaper

papier peint motif textile *m*
textile effect wallpaper

papier peint mur d'image *m*
mural wallpaper

papier peint vinyle expansé *m*
expanded vinyl wallpaper

pâte *f* paste *(see also: colle)*

patine carreaux *f* tile sheen

patine de finition *f* semi-
transparent finishing glaze

peau de chamois *f* chamois
leather

peignage *m* combing (paint
effect)

peigné -e *adj* combed (paint effect)

peigne en caoutchouc *m*
rubber comb (for combed
effect)

peigne en carton nodule *m*
corrugated card comb (for
combed effect)

peindre *v* to paint

peint -e *adj* painted

peinture *f* paint

peinture acrylique *f* acrylic
paint

peinture anti-condensation *f*
anti-condensation paint

peinture antigoutte *f* non-drip
paint

peinture bicouche *f* two-coat
paint

peinture brillant *f* gloss paint

peinture émulsion *f* emulsion
paint

peinture en aérosol *f* spray paint

peinture en flacon *f* bottle
paint (for stencils)

peinture en tube *f* tube paint
(for stencils)

peinture façade *f* masonry paint

peinture fluo *f* fluorescent paint

peinture glycéro *f* oil-based paint

peinture laquée *f* lacquier;
gloss paint

peinture mate *f* matt paint

peinture monocouche *f* one-
coat paint

peinture murale *f* wall paint

**peinture pour boiseries
intérieures** *f* interior wood paint

peinture pour plafond *f* ceiling
paint

peinture inodore *f* odourless
paint

peinture satinée *f* satin paint

perche *f* rod

pierre abrasive *f* abrasive stone

pince *f* pliers

pince coupe carrelage *f* ceramic
tile pliers

pince de carreleur *f* tiler's pliers

pinceau (*pl* -x) *f* paintbrush *(see
also: brosse)*

pinceau *m*; **pochoir** *m* stencil
brush

pinceau à glacis *m* glaze brush

pinceau de tirage *m* dragging
brush (paint effect)

**pinceau lasure, traitement
des bois** *m* stain/wood
treatment brush

pinceau plat *m* flat paintbrush

pinceau pour effet badigeon
m colourwashing brush

pinceau rond *m* round paintbrush

pinceau rond pouce *m* sash paintbrush (round-stock with rounded end to bristles)

pinceau spécial acrylique *m* acrylic paintbrush

pinceau spécial glycerol *m* paintbrush (oil-based paint)

pinceau spécial vernis *m* varnishing brush

pistolet à colle *m* glue gun

pistolet à peinture *m* paint spraygun

pistolet décapeur à air chaud *m* hot air gun

plaquette de parement *f* wall cladding

pochage *m* stippling (paint effect)

pochoir *m* stencil

poil *m* bristle (of brush)

poil synthétique *m* synthetic bristle (of a paintbrush)

polir *v* to polish

poncé -e *adj* sanded

poncer *v* to sand

poser *v* to lay

poulie *f* curtain pulley

primaire *adj* primer

pulvériser *v* to spray liquid *(see also: vaporiser)*

rabane jonc de mer *f* rush carpet

raclette à emmancher *f*; **raclette à joint** *f* rubber-blade squeegee

racloir *m* scraper/paint scraper

ralonge télescopique *f* extension handle (for roller)

râpe à céramique *f* ceramic tile file

rasoir rotatif *m* rotating razor knife

réaménager *v* to redecorate

règle à émarger *f* metal rule

règle de coup *f* cutting ruler/ metal straightedge

remplissage *m* filler

rénovateur *m* restorer

revalement *m* restoration

revêtement de sol en rouleaux vinyle *m* vinyl floorcovering (in rolls)

rideau (*pl* -x) *m* curtain -s

rideau prêt à poser *m* ready-made curtain

riflard *m* filling knife

rosace de plafond *f* ceiling rose

rouleau *m*; **roulette** *f* roller

rouleau à effet *m* texturing
roller

rouleau (*pl* **-x) à peindre** *m*
paint roller -s

rouleau à radiateur *m* radiator
roller

rouleau à vitrifier *m* varnish
roller

rouleau crépi grain fin *m* fine
grain paint effect roller

rouleau crépi gros grain *m*
coarse grain paint effect roller

rouleau de mousse
synthétique expansée *m*
synthetic foam roller

rouleau d'une polyamide
tissée *m* polyamide roller

rouleau en caoutchouc *m*
rubber roller

rouleau en mohair *m* mohair
roller

rouleau en mousse alvéolée *m*
honeycomb foam roller

rouleau en mousse floquée *m*
flocked foam roller

rouleau façade *m* exterior roller

rouleau fibres courts *m* short
fibre roller

rouleau fibres longues *m* long
fibre roller

rouleau laqueur *m* lacquering/
varnishing roller

rouleau mousse fine *m* fine
foam roller

rouleau mouton laine naturel
m natural lambswool roller

rouleau murs et plafond *m*
interior walls and ceiling roller

rouleau pour lasure *m* stain
and fluid products roller

rouleau pour les bois *m* wood
roller

rouleau rayé *m* lined roller

rouler au chiffon *v* rag rolling
(paint effect)

roulette angle nervurée *f*
ribbed roller

roulette colleur ébonite *f*
wallpaper seam roller

roulette crépi grosse grain *f*
textured paint roller

roulette d'arasement *f*
wallpaper trimming wheel *(see*
also: lame d'arasement)

roulette spécial angle *f* angled
roller

ruban adhésif de masquage *m*
masking tape

sabre de tapissier *m* palette
knife

scie à découper *f* ceramic tile saw

scie d'encadreur *f* picture frame saw

seau (*pl* -x) *m* bucket -s

seau à colle *m* paste bucket

serre-joint à cadre *m* frame clamp

seringue à colle *f* glue syringe

soie de porc *f* hog's hair bristle (of paintbrush)

sous-couche *f* undercoat

sous-couche liège isol *f* insulating cork underlay

sous-couche liège isol moquette *f* insulating cork underlay (fitted carpet)

sous-couche pour bois extérieurs *f* wood primer

spalter *m* spalter (brush for smoothing lacquer and varnish)

spatule *f* spatula

spatule à maroufler *f* paint shield

spatule crantée *f* notched spatula

store *m* blind

store à lamelles verticales *m* vertical blind

store bateau *m* roman blind

store de pergola *m*; **housse store extérieur** *f* exterior awning/pergola

store enrouleur *m* roller blind

store pour véranda *m* conservatory blind

store sur pied *m* awning with base support

store vénitien *m*; **~ à lamelles orientales** *m* venetian blind

support plafond *m* curtain ceiling bracket

support simple mural *m*; **support monobloc** *m* curtain wall bracket

table à tapissier *f* pasting table

taché -e; teinté -e *adj* stained

tacher *v* to stain

taloche *f* hawk/flat trowel; plasterer's float/hawk

tampon *m* stamp

tampon à peindre *m* paint pad

tamponnage à l'éponge *m* sponging

tamponnage et impression *m* stamping and blocking (paint effect)

tapisser *v* to wallpaper

technique de tirage *f* dragging (paint effect)

térébenthine *f* turpentine

tirage, technique de *f* dragging
   (paint effect)

toile de verre *f* glass fibre fabric

touffe *f* clump of bristles (of a
   paintbrush)

vaporiser *v* to spray as a mist
   (see also: pulvériser)

veinurage *m* wood graining
   (paint effect)

veinure *f* graining (paint effect)

verni *adj* varnished

vernis *m* varnish

vernis brillant *m* gloss varnish

vernis clair *m* clear varnish

vernis coloré *m* coloured varnish

vernis marin *m* yacht varnish

vernis mat *m* matt varnish

vernis satiné *m* satin varnish

virole *f* ferrule (of a paintbrush)

vitrificateur *f* parquet floor
   varnish

voilage *m* net curtain

voile *m* net; veil

white-spirit *m* white spirit

white-spirit inodore *m*
   odourless white spirit

NOTES

ELECTRICITE

ELECTRICITY

à piles *adj* battery operated

absorbeur *m* solar panel

accouplement *m* coupling; connection

accoupler *v* to connect

accu *m* battery

accu rechargeable *m* rechargeable battery

accumulateur *m* accumulator

actif -ive *adj* active; live

adapteur *m* adapter

adapteur européen standard *m* European standard adapter

adapteur internationaux *m* international adapter

alimentation *f* supply

alimentation de secteur *f* power supply

alimentation en électricité *f* electricity supply

alimenter *v* to supply

allumer *v* to light up; to switch on

alternateur *m* alternator

alternatif -ive *adj* alternating

amovible *adj* removable

ampérage *m* amperage

ampére *f* amp

ampèremètre *m* ammeter

ampoule *f* (light) bulb *(see also: lampe)*

ampoule, économie d'énergie *f* energy-saving light bulb

ampoule halogène *f* halogen light bulb

ampoule incadescente *f* incandescent light bulb

ampoule incadescente réflecteur *f* incandescent reflector light bulb

ampoule standard claire, culot B *f* clear incandescent light bulb (bayonet cap)

ampoule standard claire, culot E *f* clear incandescent light bulb (screw cap)

antenne *f* aerial; antenna

antiparasite *adj* anti-interference

appareil *m* appliance; device

appareil de chauffage *m* heater

appareil de commande *m* control device

appareil de mesure *m* gauge

appareillage *m* fittings; equipment

appareils éclairage extérieur *f* exterior lighting accessories

appareils très basse tension *m* ultra-low voltage accessories

appliques de salle de bain *fpl*
bathroom lighting

au sol *adj* earthed

auxiliaire *m* auxiliary

baguette *f* cable conduit

baguette sol *f* floor-fixed cable
conduit

baladeuse *f* work light

barrette *f*; **peigne**
d'alimentation *m* busbar
(consumer unit)

bas voltage *m* low voltage

basse tension *f* low voltage

batterie *f* battery

bipolaire *adj* two-pole; bipolar;
two-pin

bloc ménager *m* trailing socket

bloc multiprise *m* multiple
socket adapter

bloc multiprise extérieur *m*
exterior multiple socket adapter

boîte *f* box; mounting box

boîte à encastrer *f*; **boîte**
d'encastrement *f* recessed
mounting box

boîte à encastrer pour cloison
creuse *f* hollow partition
mounting box

boîte à encastrer pour mur
plein *f*; ~ **prise, mur plein**
f; ~ **à encastrer pour prise** *f*
solid wall mounting box

boîte à fusibles *f* fuse box

boîte appliquée *f* surface fixed
mounting box

boîte appliquée cloison sèche *f*
mounting box for partition wall

boîte avec patte de
chambranle *f* door/window
frame mounting box

boîte de dérivation *f* junction
box

boîte de distribution *f* branch
box; connection box

boîte d'encastrement à sceller
f recessed, sealed mounting box

boîte, deux ou trois postes
(interrupteurs et prises) *f*
double or triple mounting box
(switches and sockets)

boîte plafond *f* ceiling
mounting box

boîte ronde, plaque de
plâtre à encastrer *f*
round mounting box for
plasterboard wall

borne *f* terminal

borne d'arrivée *f* principal
consumer unit terminal

borne de câble *f* cable socket

borne de raccordement *f* consumer unit terminal

bouton *m* switch

bouton poussoir *m* push button

branchement *m* connection; junction; branch (wire/ conductor)

brancher *v* to connect; to link up; to plug in

broche *f* pin (of plug)

câblage *m* wiring

câblage de circuit *m* circuit wiring

câble *m* cable

câble de distribution *m* mains cable

câble de mise à la terre, cuivre nu *m*; **câblette de terre** *m* bare copper earth cable

câble électrique *m* electric cable

câble enrouler *m* cable reel

câble haut parleur, translucide, méplat *m* twin-core sheathed hi-fi flex

câble hi-fi *m* hi-fi cable

câble multifilaire *m* multi-wire cable

câble prolongateur *m* extension cable

câble rigide au mètre *m* cable by the metre (for installation in conduit)

câble rigide, bleu *m* blue PVC-sheathed cable core

câble rigide, rouge *m* red PVC-sheathed cable core

câble rigide, vert/jaune *m* green/ yellow striped PVC-sheathed cable core

câble silicone *m* silicone-sheathed cable (for use in hot atmospheres)

câble souple *m* flex

câble souple au mètre *m* flex by the metre (for installation in conduit)

câble souple en bobine *m* flex reel

câble téléphone *m* telephone cable

câble téléreport armé *m* EDF-installed cable for meter connection

câble unifilaire souple *m* PVC-sheathed flex core (not available in UK)

catégorie *f* category; class

charge *f* charge

chargeur *m* battery charger

choc électrique *m* electric shock

circuit *m* circuit

circuit fermé *m* closed circuit

clipser *v* to clip

coffret *m* box

commutateur conjoncteur *m* circuit closer

condensateur *m* capacitor

conducteur *m* conductor

conducteur actif *m* live conductor

conducteur de neutre *m* neutral conductor

conducteur de phase *m* live conductor

conducteur de protection (terre) *m* earth conductor

conducteur électrique *m* electrical conductor

conduction *f* conduction

conduit *m* conduit

connecter *v* to connect

connecteur *m* cable connector

connecteur de circuit *m* circuit connection

connecteur direct *m* flex or cable connector

connexion *f* connection

consommation *f* consumption

consommation de courant *f* current consumption

contact *m* contact

continu -e *adj* continuous

convecteur *m* convector

cordon *m* cord; lead

cordon prolongateur *m* extension lead

cosse *f* crimp connector

couleur *f* colour

coupe-câble *m* cable cutter

coupe-circuit *m*; **disjoncteur** *m* circuit breaker

coupe-circuit à broche *m* fuse holder (porcelain fuses)

coupe-circuit à fusible *m* fused circuit breaker

coupe-fil *m* wire cutter

couper *v* to cut; to switch off

couper le courant *v* to cut off the power

couplage *m* connection

couplage en série *m* series connection

coupler *v* to connect

coupler en parallèle *v* to connect in parallel

coupler en série *v* to connect in series

coupure *f* cut; power cut; disconnection

courant *m* current; power

courant alternatif *m*
alternating current (a.c.)

courant basse tension *m* low
voltage current

courant de regime *m* normal
current

courant direct *m* direct current
(d.c.)

court-circuit *m* short circuit

court-circuiter *v* to short circuit

couteau d'électricien *m*
handyman's knife (nearest
equivalent)

couvercle dérivation *m*
junction box cover

cuisinière *f* cooker

cuivre *m* copper

culot B *m* bayonet cap (light bulb)

culot E *m* screw cap (light bulb)

déclencher *v* to trip

déclencher un circuit *v* to break
a circuit

déclencheur *m* trip

déconnecter *v* to disconnect

défaillance *f* breakdown;
failure; fault

défaut *m* fault

délester *v* to cut off power from

démarrer *v* to switch on
(appliance)

dépense *f* consumption

dérivation *f* junction

dériver *v* to divert

**dés de raccordement
(dominos)** *m* connector block

détecteur *m* detector; detection
device

détecteur de câbles *m* cable
detector

**détecteur de coupure de
courant** *m* electrical current
cut detector

détecteur de fumée *m* smoke
detector

détecteur de gel *m* frost
detector

détecteur d'inondation *m* flood
detector

**détecteur de monoxide de
carbone** *m* carbon monoxide
detector

détecteur de mouvement *m*
movement detector (alarm system)

**détecteur d'ouverture ou de
chocs** *m* break-in detector
(alarm system)

**détecteur de panne de
congélateur** *m* freezer alarm

détecteur technique *m*
specialist detector

disjoncteur *m* circuit breaker; trip switch

disjoncteur différentiel *m* residual current device (RCD)

disjoncteur divisionnaire différentiel *m* miniature circuit breaker (MCB)

douille *f* lampholder

douille à baïonnette *f* bayonet bulb socket

douille à vis *f* screw bulb socket

douille double bague *f* lampholder (two retaining rings)

douille laiton *f* brass lampholder

douille simple bague *f* lampholder (one retaining ring)

dynamo *f* dynamo; generator

éclairage *f* lighting

éclairage automatique *f* automatic lighting

écoulement *m* flow; leakage

écoulement d'électricité *m* flow of electricity

EDF (Electricité de France) French electricity supply company

électricité *f* electricity

électrification *f* electrification

électrique *adj* electric; electrical

électromagnétique *adj* electromagnetic

électrostatique *adj* electrostatic

élément *m* component; element; unit

embout de câble *m* cable terminal/termination

enclencher *v* to engage; to switch on (appliance)

enduit étanche *m* sealant

enfiler *v* to thread

équipement *m* equipment; fittings

étanche *adj* waterproof; watertight

faire masse *v* to act as earth

fermer *v* to close

fermer *v* **un circuit** to close a circuit

fiche *f* plug

fiche caoutchouc *f* rubber plug

fiche de connexion *f* connector plug

fiche deux P+T (phase, terre) *f* two-pin plug (live, earth)

fiche électrique *f* electric plug

fiche femelle *f* female plug

fiche mâle *f* male plug

fiche mâle/femelle deux P+T (phase, terre) *f* male/female plug (live, earth)

fiche mâle/femelle deux pôles *f* two-pole male/female plug

fiche trois P+N+T (phase, neutre, terre) *f* three-pin plug (live, neutral, earth)

fil *m* wire; thread; filament

fil conducteur *m* cable core

fil de phase *m* live wire

fil de plomb *m* fuse wire

fil hors courant *m* dead wire

fil neutre *m* neutral wire

fil nu *m* bare wire

fondre un fusible *v* to blow a fuse

foudre *f* lightning

fréquence *f* frequency

fusible *m* fuse

fusible à cartouche *m* cartridge fuse

fusible bon *m* fuse intact

fusible céramique *m* ceramic fuse

fusible grillé *m* burnt out fuse

fusible principal *m* main fuse

fusible tabatière *m* fuse box

gaine *f* corrugated flexible cable sheathing

gaine de protection *f* protection sheathing

gaine plastique rigide *f* plastic rigid sheathing

gaine précâblée *f* sheathing with pre-installed circuit cable

gaine préfilée *f* sheathing with pre-installed cable cores

générateur *m* generator

grille *f* grill; grid

griller *v* to blow; to burn out

haute tension *m* high voltage

hertz *m* hertz

hors courant *adj* dead; no current

horloge de programmation hebdomadaire *f* time clock, 7-day

horloge de programmation journalier *f* time clock, 24-hour

intensité *f* intensity

interphone radio *m* intercom

interrompre *v* to interrupt; to cut out

interrupteur *m* switch

interrupteur à pied *m* foot-operated switch

interrupteur bipolaire *m* two-pole switch

interrupterur combiné pac saillie *m* surface-mounted switch

interrupteur de contrôle *m* control switch

interrupteur différentiel *m* consumer unit main switch

interrupteurs et prises à distance *m* remote control switches and sockets

isolant *m*; **isolateur** *m* insulator

isolant -e *adj*; **isolateur** *adj* insulating

isolation *f*; **isolement** *m* insulation

joule *m* joule

lampadaire *m* standard lamp

lampe *f* lamp; bulb *(see also: ampoule)*

lampe de poche *f* battery torch

lampe halogène TBTS (très basse tension) *f* extra-low voltage halogen light bulb

lampe standard claire *f* clear light bulb

lampe standard dépolie *f* pearl/opal light bulb

lampe témoin *f* pilot light

lave-linge *m* washing machine

lave-vaisselle *m* dishwasher

mesure *f* measurement

mesurer *v* to measure

mettre *v* to put

mettre à terre *v* to earth

minuterie *f* timeswitch

mise à la terre *v* earth; earthing

montage électrique *m* circuit diagram

moulure *f* surface-mounted PVC moulding (for passage of electric cables); casing

neutre *adj* neutral

nominal -e (pl -aux) *adj* nominal

norme *f* standard

nu -e *adj* bare

ohm *m* ohm

ohmmètre *m* ohmmeter

omnipolaire *adj* all poles

parafoudre *m*; **paratonnerre** *m* lightning rod

parafoudre modulaire *m*; **paratonnerre** *m* anti-lightning protector

phase *f* live

pile *f* battery

pince *f* pliers; pincers

pince à dénuder à becs *f* side-cutting wirestrippers

pince à dénuder automatique *f* multiple jaw wirestrippers

181

pince à dénuder réglable *f*
adjustable wirestrippers

pince coupante *f* wirecutters

pince crocodile *f* crocodile clip

pince de fixation *f* clip

piquet de terre *m* earthing spike

**plaquette fusible à fil de
laiton** *f* brass fuse wire holder
(old-type; no UK equivalent)

point lumineux *m* light fitting

polarité *f* polarity

pôle *m* pole

pôle moins *m* minus pole

pôle négatif *m* negative pole

pôle plus *m* plus pole

pôle positif *m* positive pole

porte-fusible *m* fuse holder

poser *v* to put in place

poussoir à voyant *m* push
switch

prise *f* socket

prise à encastrer plinthe *f*
recessed skirting board socket

prise de courant *f* power point

prise de terre *f* two-hole socket
with earth pin

prise deux P+T *f* two-hole
socket plus earth

prise digitale *f* programmable
digital switch

prise double deux pôles *f*
double two-pole socket

prise électrique *f* electrical socket
outlet

prise en appliqué *f* surface-
mounted socket

prise murale *f* wall socket

prise programmable *f*
programmable switch

prise téléphone *f* telephone
socket

prise téléphone/informatique
f telephone/computer socket

prise TV/FM/SAT *f* television/
stereo/satellite socket

prise trois P+T *f* three-hole
socket plus earth

programmateur mécanique
f programmable mechanical
switch

projecteur *m* spotlight

**projecteur halogène sur
trépied télescopique** *m*
halogen spotlight on telescopic
tripod

projecteur portable *m* portable
spotlight

prolongateur-adapteur *m*
adapter on extension lead

protection *f* protection

protection anti-foudre
f lightning voltage surge
protector

puissance *f* power; wattage

raccordement *m* connecting;
connection joining

raccorder *v* to connect; to
connect up; to join; to couple

ralonge *m* extension cable

réflecteur dépolie *f* pearl/opal
reflector light bulb

relais *m* relay

répartir *v* to distribute

répartition *f* distribution

réseau *m* network; system; grid

réseau d'éclairage *m* lighting
system

réseau électrique *m* electrical
system/network

résistance *f* resistance

rétablir *v* re-establish

rétablir le courant *v* to put
power back on again

sans fil *adj* cordless; wireless

schéma *m* diagram; scheme

serre-câble à cheville *m* cable
clip with screw fitting

socle *m* lamp base

sonnerie *f* doorbell

sonnerie d'alarme *f* alarm bell

sortie câble *f* cable exit

source *f* source

source d'énergie *f* source of
energy

spot *m* spotlight

spot halogène *m* halogen
spotlight

surintensité *f* overcurrent

surtension *f* overvoltage

survoltage *m* boosting

**tableau de commande
principal** *m* main switch
board

tableau de commutateurs *m*
switchboard

tableau de fusibles *m* fuse board

tableau de répartition *m*
consumer unit

**tableau électrique, coffret
vide** *m* consumer unit casing

tableau pré-équipé *m*
consumer unit pre-fitted with
MCBs and RCD

tension *f* voltage

tension du secteur *f* mains
voltage

tension maximale *f* maximum
voltage

terre *f* earth

testeur de fusibles *m* fuse tester

thermostat *m* thermostat

tire-fils *f* pull-cord for installing
cables in sheathing

tournevis *m* screwdriver

tournevis d'électricien *m*
electrician's screwdriver

tournevis pour vis Phillips *m*
Phillips screwdriver

tournevis testeur *m* tester
screwdriver

transformateur *m* transformer

transmission *f* transmission

triplite *m* triple socket adapter

tripolaire *adj* triple pole;
tripolar

tube fluorescent *m* fluorescent
tube

unifilaire *adj* single wire

unipolaire *adj* single pole

variateur interrupteur *m* dimmer
switch

volt *m* volt

voltage *m* voltage

voltmètre *m* voltmeter

watt *m* watt

wattmètre *m* wattmeter

NOTES

FINANCIER

FINANCIAL

BANKING
TAX
INSURANCE

agio *m* bank charge

ancien solde *f* previous balance

assurance *f* insurance

assurance supplémentaire *f* supplementary insurance

assurance-vie *f* life insurance

assuré -e *adj* insured

assuré -e *mf* insured party

s'assurer *v* to take out insurance for oneself

assureur *m* insurer

bancaire *adj* banking

banque *f* bank

chèque *m* cheque

chèque de banque *m* banker's draft

chèque sans provision *m* bounced cheque

chéquier *m* cheque book

code confidentiel *m* PIN number

code guichet *m* branch code

compte *m* account

compte à terme *m* deposit account

compte bancaire *m* bank account

compte courant *m*; **compte de dépôts** *m* current account

compte de dépôt joint *m* joint current account

compte d'épargne *m* savings account

compte débiteur *m* overdrawn account

contracter une assurance *v* to take out an insurance policy

crédit hypothécaire *m* mortgage

crédit relais *m* bridging loan; finance

débit *m* debit

découvert *m* overdraft

dépôt *m* deposit

endosser *v* to endorse (the back of a cheque)

faire assurer *v* to insure

guichet *m* bank counter

guichet automatique *m* automated teller machine (ATM)

impôt *m* tax *(see also: taxe)*

monnaie *f* coins; change

mutuelle *f* mutual insurance company

prélèvement *m* direct debit

prêt personnel *m* personal loan

reçu *m* receipt

rejeter un chèque *v* to bounce a cheque

relevé de compte *m*; **extrait** *m* bank statement

relevé d'identité bancaire (RIB) *m* bank identity record

remise *f* remittance

retrait d'argent *m* withdrawal of money

retrait d'espèces *m* cash withdrawal

sécurité sociale *f* public health insurance

solde *f* balance of account

taux de change *m* exchange rate

taxe *m* tax *(see also: impôt)*

taxe foncière *f* property tax

taxe habitation *f* habitation tax

virement *m* bank transfer

NOTES

QUINCAILLERIE

IRONMONGERY

ADHESIVES
WEATHERPROOFING
WALLPLUGS & FIXINGS
SECURITY

abattant (d'un siège-toilette) *m* toilet seat

adhésif *m* adhesive *(see also: colle)*

adhésif anti-dérapant *m* anti-slip adhesive tape

adhésif anti-fuites *m* leak repair adhesive tape

adhésif de masquage courbe protection *m* protective adhesive tape (corners and curves)

adhésif double face *m* double-sided adhesive tape

adhésif double face extérieur *m* double-sided exterior grade adhesive tape

adhésif double face extra fort *m* extra strong double-sided adhesive tape

adhésif double face miroirs *m* mirror fixing double-sided adhesive tape

adhésif double face multi-usages *m* multi-purpose double-sided tape

adhésif emballage *m* packaging tape

adhésif masquage droit protection *m* protective adhesive tape (straight edges)

adhésif pour aluminium *m* aluminium adhesive tape

adhésif protection toutes peintures bois/murs/peints *m;* **~ protection toutes peintures vitres/carrelages** *m* masking tape

adhésif PVC rigide pour laine de roche/laine de verre *m* PVC adhesive tape (mineral fibre and glass fibre insulation)

adhésif PVC souple *m* soft PVC adhesive tape

adhésif PVC souple multi-usages *m* all-purpose soft PVC adhesive tape

adhésif raccord plaques de plâtre *m* plasterboard jointing adhesive tape

adhésif réparer/renforcer *m* reparing and reinforcing adhesive tape

adhésif toile *m* canvas-backed adhesive tape

adhésif translucide *m* translucent adhesive tape

agrafe *f* hook

agrafe à T *f* T-clamp

alarme *f* alarm

alarme à déclenchement magnétique *f* magnetic door alarm

alarme autonome *f* autonomous alarm

alarme autonome infrarouge *f* infrared motion detector alarm

alarme de fenêtre *f* window alarm

alarme pour porte *f* door alarm

alliage *f* alloy

ancre en forme d'un S *m* S-plate

anneau brisé *m* split ring

antenne *f* antenna

arbre *m* axle

armoire de rangement métal *f* metal tool storage cupboard

arrêt de volet entrebâilleur *m* shutter stay

arrêt de volet avec poignée *m* shutter stay (with handle)

attache de fixation *f* fixing clip

avertisseur d'entrée *m* entry alarm

bague *f* ring

baladeur à outils *m* portable tool bag

balai-toilette *m* toilet brush

baraque de chantier *f* builder's roller cabinet

barillet *m* cylinder lock

barre antipanique coupe feu *f* anti-bolt cutter security bar

barre de sécurité *f* security bar

barre de sécurité pour persienne *f* security bar (louvre shutter)

barre de sécurité pour volet *f* security bar (shutter)

bas de porte *m* excluder strip (draught/rain/sound)

bas de porte à bavette *m* flapped door strip

bas de porte à lèvres *m* lipped door strip

bas de porte argent (brosse dure) *m* silver heavy-duty brush door strip

bas de porte bronze (brosse dure) *m* bronze heavy-duty brush door strip

bas de porte brosse *m* brush door strip

bas de porte brosse souple *m* soft brush door strip

bas de porte de garage grande bavette *m* large thermoplastic flap seal (garage)

bas de porte eau/air/bruit adhésif *m* adhesive door

strip (rain deflector/draught
excluder/sound insulator)

bas de porte garage brosse *m*
brush door strip (garage)

**bas de porte garage petite
bavette** *m* small thermoplastic
flap seal (garage)

bas de porte pivotant *m*
pivoting door strip

bâton colle pour cuir *m* leather
glue stick

bâton colle pour métaux *m*
metal glue stick

**bâton colle pour sanitaire/
câbles/matériaux poreux**
m bathroom/cables/porous
materials glue stick

**bâton colle pour textile et
liège** *m* textiles and cork glue
stick

bâton de colle *m*; ~ **colle** *m*
glue stick

bâton de colle multi-usage *m*
all-purpose glue stick

**bâton de colle pour bois
et dérivés** *m* wood and
derivatives glue stick

**bâton de colle pour joints
et faïence** *m* joints and
earthenware glue stick

**bâton de colle pour
matériaux sensibles à la
chaleur** *m* heat sensitive
materials glue stick

**bâton de colle pour PVC et
câbles** *m* PVC and cables glue
stick

batterie *f*; **pile** *f* battery (toys,
watches etc.)

boîte aux lettres *f* letter box

**boîtier autoprotege (avec
serrure à clef impulsion)**
m anti-tamper case (with
keyswitch and key)

boulon *m* bolt (hardware)

boulon à clavette *m* cotter bolt

boulon à croc *m* hook bolt

boulon à écrou *m* screw bolt

boulon à tête carrée *m* square-
head bolt

boulon à tête fraisée *m*
countersunk-head bolt

boulon à tête ronde *m* round-
head bolt

boulon d'ancrage *m* anchor
bolt

boulon d'assemblage *m*
assembling bolt

boulon de fondation *m*
foundation bolt

boulon de retenue *m*
retaining bolt

boulonnerie *f* nuts and bolts

bourrelet *m* foam draught strip

bourrelet *m*; **joint de calfeutrage** *m* weatherstrip

bouton *m* knob

bouton de sonnette *m* doorbell

bouton de tirage *m* door knob

bouton moleté *m* milled knob

bouton panique sans fil *m*
wireless panic button

bouton poussoir d'appel *m*
doorbell button

bride de renfort *f* lock
reinforcement bar

broche *f* spike

buse pour pistolet à colle *f*
glue gun nozzle

butée de porte *f* doorstop

cadenas à clef *m* padlock

cadenas à combinaisons *m*
combination lock

cadenas à combinaisons programmable *m*
programmable combination lock

cadenas anse haute *m* long
shackle padlock

cadenas anse protégée *m*
closed shackle padlock

cadenas laiton haute sécurité *m* high security brass padlock

cadenas laiton massif *m* solid
brass padlock

cadenas laminé *m* laminated
padlock

caisse à outils sur roulettes *f*
wheeled tool box

caisse métallique à plateau *f*
articulated trays metal case

calfeutrage *m* draughtproofing

cantine renforcée *f* reinforced
toolchest

carillon *m* door chime

carillon sans fil portée *m*
portable wireless door chime

ceinture porte-outil *f* tool belt

cellule de détection infrarouge *f* infrared
detection cell

cellule photoélectrique *f*
photocell

centrale-sirène intégrée *f*
integrated siren

chaînette de sécurité *f* door
chain

chariot à roulettes *m* wheeled
trolley

charnière à ressort *f* spring
hinge

charnon *m* hinge knuckle

cheville *f* wallplug; pin

cheville à frapper *f* hammer-in plug

cheville anti-effraction indémontable *f* security grille plug

cheville autoforeuse *f* self-drilling fixing

cheville autoforeuse à bascule *f* self-drilling plasterboard fixing

cheville autoforeuse en acier à visser *f* self-screwing steel fixing

cheville autoforeuse vix cadre *f* self-drilling fixing (frames and plasterboard)

cheville en acier *f* steel plug

cheville en acier à bascule *f* toggle fixing for ceiling; ~ **avec crochet pour éclairage et suspension** *f* (with suspension hook); ~ **avec piton pour éclairage et suspension** *f* (with suspension eye); ~ **avec vis pour éclairage et suspension** *f* (with suspension screw)

cheville en acier à ressort *f* steel spring toggle cavity fixing

~ **avec crochet** *f* (with hook); ~ **avec piton** *f* (with eye); ~ **avec vis** *f* (with screw)

cheville en fonte *f* cast iron wallplug

cheville en laiton fendue pour plafond suspendu *f* expanding brass plug (suspended ceiling)

cheville métallique *f* anchor fixing

cheville métallique à expansion *f* hollow wall anchor

cheville métallique et vis *f* anchor fixing with screw

cheville mini *f* mini hammer-in plug

cheville nylon *f* nylon plug

cheville nylon à clouer *f* hammer-in nylon plug

cheville nylon à expansion *f* nylon anchor fixing

cheville nylon à expansion avec vis *f* nylon anchor fixing with screw

cheville nylon à expansion sans vis *f* nylon anchor fixing without screw

cheville nylon à visser *f* nylon block fixing plug

cheville nylon fendue *f*
expanding nylon plug

**cheville nylon fendue pour
encadrement de portes et
fenêtres** *f* nylon frame fixing
plug (doors and windows)

**cheville nylon spécial béton
cellulaire** *f* nylon plug
(breezeblocks)

cheville plaque de plâtre *f*
plasterboard plug (hollow wall
anchor)

cheville universelle *f* universal
wallplug

clavier de codage *m* code
keypad (alarm)

clé *f* key

clou tapissier *m* upholstery
pin

coffre de chantier fixe *m*
builder's tool box

coffre-fort *m* safe

coffre-fort à encastrer *m* wall
safe

coin *m* corner

colle *f* glue *(see also: adhésif)*

colle à bois polyuréthane *f*
polyurethane wood glue

coffre à clés *m*; **armoire à clé** *f*
key cabinet

**colle à froid de rêvetement
bitume** *f* cold process adhesive
(for bitumen)

coffre à outils *m*; **boîte à outils** *f*
tool box

colle acrylique pour puzzle *f*
jigsaw puzzle glue

**colle acrylique pour sous-
couche** *f* acrylic underlay
adhesive

colle bois prise rapide *f* rapid-
setting wood adhesive

colle carrelage pâte *f* ceramic
tile adhesive

**colle cyanoacrylate
porcelaine et faïence** *f*
cyanoacrylate glue (porcelain
and earthenware)

colle de blocage *f* gap-filling
adhesive

colle en pâte *f* adhesive paste

colle époxy *f* epoxy glue

colle epoxy acier seringue *f*
epoxy adhesive steel syringe

colle époxy pour bois *f* epoxy
wood glue

colle époxy pour métal *f*
epoxy metal glue

colle époxy pour verre *f* epoxy
glass glue

colle époxy universelle *f* epoxy universal glue

colle fibres de verre et revêtements textiles muraux *f* fibreglass and textile wallcovering adhesive

colle fix facile tous supports *f* all-purpose easy fixing adhesive

colle isolants mince polystyrène expansé *f* expanded polystyrene panel adhesive

colle isolants mince polystyrène extrudé *f* extruded polystyrene panel adhesive

colle latex naturel pour tissu *f* latex textile adhesive

colle murale liège *f* cork wall tile adhesive

colle murale universelle *f* interior wall adhesive

colle néoprène liquide *f* neoprene liquid glue

colle néoprène pour manchon d'isolation *f* neoprene pipe lagging adhesive

colle ni-clou ni-vis *f* nailless/screwless adhesive; ~ **extrême cartouche** *f* (cartridge); ~ **tube** *f* (tube)

colle papiers intissés *f* non-woven wallcovering paste

colle papier peints *f* wallpaper paste

colle papier peints universelle *f* universal wallpaper paste

colle papier peints vinyls *f* vinyl wallpaper paste

colle plastique *f* plastic adhesive

colle polymère universelle *f* polymer glue

colle polystyrène *f* polystyrene glue

colle polystyrène phonicolle *f* polystyrene soundproofing adhesive (not available in UK)

colle pour cuir et caoutchouc *f* leather and rubber adhesive

colle pour dalles de plafond *f* ceiling tile adhesive

colle pour frises décoratives *f* decorative frieze adhesive

colle pour joint de foyers et inserts *f* fire cement

colle pour liège sol et mur *f* cork adhesive (floor and wall)

colle pour maquette *f* model glue

colle pour miroirs *f* mirror adhesive

colle pour papiers peints épais *f* thick wallpaper adhesive

colle pour plaquettes et parement *f* wallboard adhesive

colle pour plastique rigide *f* rigid plastic adhesive

colle pour PVC raccords et gouttières rigide *f* PVC joint and guttering adhesive

colle pour rosaces et corniches *f* ceiling rose and cornice adhesive

colle pour rosaces et moulures vinyles et expansées *f* ceiling rose and moulding adhesive

colle pour rouleaux isolants *f* insulating roll adhesive

colle pour stratifié et flottant *f* laminate and floating floor adhesive

colle pour textiles muraux *f* textile wallcovering adhesive

colle pour tissu *f* fabric glue

colle pour toile de verre *f* fibreglass fabric adhesive

colle PVC *f* PVC glue

colle renforcée frises *f* reinforced frieze adhesive

colle renforcée revêtements textiles muraux et toiles de verre *f* reinforced textile wallcoverings and fibre glass fabric adhesive

colle repositionnable spécial pochoir *f* repositionable stencil glue

colle résine époxydique *f* epoxy resin adhesive

colle sans solvant *f* solvent-free adhesive

colle silicone *f* silicone adhesive

colle sol polyvalente *f* multi-purpose flooring adhesive

colle sols plastiques et moquettes *f* plastic flooring and carpet adhesive

colle spécial parquet *f* parquet fooring adhesive

colle textile *f* textile glue

colle transparente après séchage *f* transparent drying adhesive

colle universelle instantanée *f* superglue

colle universelle instantanée, 'easy brush' flacon *f*

superglue with brush applicator

colle universelle repositionnable *f* repositionable adhesive

colle vinylique *f* vinyl glue

colle vinylique pour bois extérieur *f* vinyl adhesive (exterior wood)

colle vinylique pour bois intérieur *f* vinyl adhesive (interior wood)

colle vinylique pour papier et carton *f* vinyl adhesive (paper and cardboard)

collet *m* collar

combine audio supplémentaire *m* handset/receiver

commande à clé *f* keyswitch

compartiment *m* compartment

condamnation *f* locking device

console métallique *f* metal bracket

console murale *f* wall bracket

contact de porte supplémentaire pour alarme *m* wired alarm system door contact

contacteur de porte *m* door contact

contrôle d'accès carte magnétique *m* magnetic card access control (security)

coquille *f* bearing

coulisse *f* runner; slider

coulisse de tiroir *f* drawer runner

coulisseau à frein réglable *m* sliding stay with adjustable stop

crémaillère *f* shutter retaining hook

crémone *f* window catch

crochet à tableau *m* picture hook

crochet porte-outils *m* tool wall hook

cylindre de serrure *m* lock cylinder

détecteur à cellule photoélectrique *m* photoelectric detector

détecteur contact de sol *m* floor contact detector

détecteur de bris de glace *m* glass break detector

détecteur de choc (fenêtre) *m* shock detector (windows)

détecteur de coupure secteur *m* appliance alarm (radio transmitted)

détecteur de fumée *m* smoke detector

détecteur de gaz *m* gas detector

détecteur de movement *m* movement detector

dessous de porte *m* door roll draught excluder

détecteur perivolumetrique alarme électrique *m* air pressure sensor dectector (security)

détecteur special animaux domestiques *m* pet immune motion detector

déverrouillage externe *m* exterior door lock

éclairage de sécurité *m* security lighting

écrou *m* nut; ~ **borgne** *m* blind nut; ~ **à six pans** *m* hexagonal nut ~ **de blocage** *m* locking nut; ~ **carré** *m* square nut; ~ **ordinaire** *m* standard nut; ~ **à oreilles** *m* wing nut

ensemble cheville et pince *m* plug and insertion tool set

entrebâilleur *m* door guard/ chain

entrebâilleur de fenêtre *m* window restrictor

entrebâilleur de volet *m* shutter restrictor

équerre *f* set square

équerre d'angle *f* angle plate; corner plate

équipement *m* fitments

espagnolette crémone *f* French window locking bolt

fer *m* bit; iron

fer d'angle *m* L-iron

ferme-porte *m* door closer

ferme-porte à ressort *f* spring door closer

ferme-porte à ressort spirale *f* self closing gate spring

ferme-porte automatique *f* automatic door closer

ferrure *f* hinge; iron fittings

ferrure de volet *f* shutter hinge

fixation néoprène cartouche *f* neoprene fixing glue

fixer mousse double face *m* adhesive foam pad

gâche *f* striking plate (lock); wall hook

gond *m* **et penture** *f* hook and hinge

gorge *f* tumbler (lock)

grille de défense *f* security grille

halogène électrique radar *f*
electric halogen security light

interrupteur *m* control switch

interrupteur crépusculaire *m*
infrared sensor

**joint adhésif caoutchouc profil
«E»** *m* E-profile weatherstrip

**joint adhésif caoutchouc
profil «P»** *m* adhesive rubber
P-profile weatherstrip

**joint adhésif longue durée
combles** *m* long-lasting
adhesive foam weatherstrip

**joint adhésif portes et
fenêtres PVC** *m* adhesive
PVC weatherstrip (doors and
windows)

joint fenêtres petites rainures *m*
grooved weatherstrip (windows)

joint mousse universel *m* foam
weatherstrip

**joint pour revêtements
plastiques et vinyliques** *m*
epoxy plastics and vinyl glue

judas *m* door viewer

kit alarme sans fil *m* wireless
home alarm system kit

**kit alarme sans fil
appartement** *m* apartment
alarm system kit

kit alarme sans fil compact *m*
compact alarm kit

kit motorisation porte garage
m garage door automation kit

lame de scie à métaux *f*
hacksaw blade

lampe détecteur infrarouge *f*
infrared detector security light

lampe électrique éclairage *f*
electric security light

loquet *m* latch

malle *f* chest

mallette *f* small case

**mallette de chevilles
autoforeuses** *f* case of self-
drilling fixings

marteau (*pl* **-x) de porte** *m*
door knocker

mastic colle *m* mastic adhesive

mastic colle auto/marine *m*
auto/marine mastic adhesive

**mastic colle verre-vitrage
cartouche** *m* glass and
window mastic adhesive

moniteur video *m* video
monitor

**mortier adhésif (pour plaque
de plâtre et doublage)**
m adhesive mortar (for
plasterboard)

motorisation de portail *f* gate automation

motorisation de volet *f* shutter automation

œillet *m* eyelet

ouvre-volet *m* shutter opener

paire de renfort paumelles *m* reinforcing security hinge bolt

paire de verrous *m* locking bar (top and bottom of door)

panneau mural alvéolé *m* toolboard wall panel

pastilles adhésives *f* self-adhesive pads

pâte à coller *f* moldable adhesive

paumelle *f* split hinge

pêne *m*; **verrou** *m* bolt (lock)

pêne dormant *m* deadbolt

piquet *m* stake

pistolet à colle *m* glue gun

pistolet à colle à basse température *m* low melt glue gun

pistolet à colle avec sélecteur de température *m* variable temperature glue gun

pistolet à colle haute température *m* high temperature hot melt glue gun

pistolet à colle sans fil *m* cordless glue gun

pitonnerie *f* hooks and eyes

pivot *m* pivot

plaque de protection *f* cover plate

plaque de renfort *f* reinforcing plate

plaque en tôle *f* sheet iron cover

poignée d'ameublement *f* furniture handle

poignée de porte *f* door handle

poignée verrou de sécurité volet bois *f* locking bar (wooden shutters)

pointe à placage *f* veneer pin

porte-cadenas *m* hasp and staple

porte-outils magnétique *m* magnetic wall tool rack

porte-rouleau *m* toilet roll holder

portier électronique *m* entryphone/intercom

presse d'angle *f* angle clamp

profilé en T *m* T-iron

punaise *f* drawing pin

rangement des outils *m* tool storage

ressort à boudin *m* spiral spring

rivet *m* rivet

rivet à tête ronde *m* round-headed rivet

rondelle *f* washer

rondelle à denture *f* serrated washer

rondelle carrossier *f* large washer

rondelle Grower *f* split washer

rondelle plate *f* flat washer

rosace *f*; ~ **à clé** *f* escutcheon plate

rosace avec entrée de clé *f* escutcheon with keyhole

roulante de chantier *f* builder's roller cabinet

rouleau *m* runner

roulette *f* castor

ruban adhésif *m* adhesive tape

sécurité *f* security

seringue à colle *f* glue syringe

serre-joint *m* joiner's clamp

serrure *f* lock

serrure à appliquer horizontale *f* horizontal surface-mounted lock

serrure à appliquer verticale *f* vertical surface-mounted lock

serrure à bandeau *f* multipoint locking bar

serrure à ressort *f* latch lock; spring lock

serrure bas de porte *f* base door lock

serrure électronique à contrôle accès *f* electronic combination lock

serrure en applique *f* surface-mounted lock

serrure encastrée *f* mortise lock

serrure encastrer à clé *f* mortise deadlock

serrure haut de porte *f* top door lock

serrure multipoints *f* multipoint lock

serrure quatre gorges *f* four tumbler lock

serrure trois points *f* three-point locking bar

serrure trois points horizontale à tirage *f* multipoint rim lock

serrure tubulaire *f* tubular lock

servante *f* roller cabinet

sirène/flash factice *f* dummy siren/light

support *m* support

targette *f* door bolt

télécommande *f* remote control

tige filetée *f* threaded stem (door handle)

transmetteur de signal sans fil *m* wireless signal transmitter (alarm)

**transmetteur téléphonique
blindé** *m* armoured radio
alarm transmitter

trou de cylinder *m* keyhole

trousse *f* tool roll

valise alu *f* aluminium case

verrou à coquille *m* barrel bolt

verrou à plaquer *m* slide bolt

verrou à ressort *m* spring bolt

**verrou antipince-doigts
pour volet roulant** *m*
security bolt (roller shutter)

verrou automatique *m* moving
bar and turn button rim lock

verrou clé et bouton *m* keylock
and turn button rim lock

verrou de fermeture *m*
locking bolt

verrou de sécurité portail *m*
gate security bar

verrou double entrée *m*
double input lock

verrou haute sécurité *m* high
security bolt

verrou sûreté à bouton *m*
night latch (with moving bar)

vidéo surveillance *m* video
surveillance

NOTES

FERRONNERIE

METALWORK

METALWORK
ENGINEERING
MECHANICS
WELDING

abrasif carbure de silicium *m*
silicon carbide paper

abrasif corindon *m* corundum
paper

acétylène *m* acetylene (gas
welding)

acier *m* steel

acier galvanisé *m* galvanised
steel

allume-brûleur *m* cup lighter
(gas welding)

aluminium *m* aluminium

anti-retour pare flame *m*
flashback arrestor (gas welding)

**baguette de brasage cuivre,
phosphore, argent** *f* silver,
phosphorous, copper brazing
rod

baguette de brasure *f*; **~ de
soudure** *f* brazing rod

**baguette de métal d'apport et
étain** *f* welding rod

baguette de soudure arc *f* arc
welding brazing rod

barre en métal *f* metal bar

barre plat métal *f* flat metal bar

barre ronde serrurier *f*
round metal bar

**brasure aluminium
basse température** *f* low
temperature aluminium
brazing rod

batte de tôlier-carrossier *f* panel
beater

**bobine de souder soudure
étain** *f* bobbin of tin solder

bobine fourré *f* MIG welding
wire on bobbin

**bobine fourré pour poste sans
gaz** *f* gasless MIG wire on bobbin

bouchons d'oreille *mpl*;
boulequies *fpl* ear plugs

bouteille gaz rechargeable *f*
refillable gas bottle

bronze *m* bronze

brûleur *m* burner

brûleur à bec plat *m* flat beak
burner

**brûleur à flamme
enveloppante** *m* enveloping
burner

brûleur à pointe super fine *m*
extra fine point burner

brûleur grande flamme *m*
large flame burner

burin de mécanicien *m* cold
chisel

buse *f* shroud (MIG welder)

buse de soudage *f* welding
nozzle

butane *m* butane

caisse mécanicien *f* mechanic's
toolbox

calibre d'épaisseur *m* feeler
gauge

carré *f* square section iron

cartouche jetable *f* disposable
gas bottle

casque anti-bruit *m* ear
defenders

chalumeau *m* gas welding/
soldering/cutting torch

chalumeau bi-gaz *m* two gases
welding kit

chalumeau chauffeur *m*
heating torch

chalumeau coupeur *m* cutting
torch (gas welding)

chalumeau monogaz *m* gas
torch

chalumeau soudeur *m* welding
torch

chariot *m* cylinder trolley (gas
welding)

clé *f* spanner

clé à molette *f* monkey wrench;
adjustable spanner

clé à pipe *f* box or socket spanner

clé à pipe débouchée *f* through
box spanner

clé cliquet *f* speed wrench

clé étoile *f* star key

clé mâle *f* hexagonal key

clé mixte *f* combination spanner

coffret de tarauds et filières *m*
tap and die set

compas à pointes sèches *m*
spring divider

compas d'épaisseur *m* outside
spring calliper

cornière *f* angle iron

cornière égale *f* angle iron,
equal

cornière inégale *f* angle iron,
unequal

coupe-boulons *mpl* bolt cutters

cuivre *m* copper

débilitre à colonne *f* gas flow
meter

décapant *m* flux

détendeur *m* regulator

disque à lamelles *m* flap disk

disque à tronçonner *m* cutting
disk

disque drap à polir tissu libre
m buffing wheel

disque sisal *m* sisal polishing disk

douille *f* socket spanner

économiseur de gaz *m* gas
economiser

écran thermique *m* anti-thermic screen (gas welding)

électrode *f* electrode (arc welder/MIG welder)

électrode enrobée *f* fluxed electrode (arc welder)

équerre acier *f* steel square

équerre alu *f* aluminium square

équerre simple à 90° (quatre-vingt-dix degrés) *f* square

ergoscie *f* keyhole saw

étau *m* vice

fer à souder électronique *m* electric soldering iron

feuille abrasive *f* abrasive sheet

fil *m* wire

fil acier *m* mild steel wire

fil fourré acier sans gaz *m* gasless MIG wire

fil massif *m* solid wire

foret *m* drill bit

foret HSS *m* high speed steel (HSS) drill bit

foret métaux queue hexag *m* hexagonal shank metal drill bit

foret métaux queue réduite *m* reduced shank metal drill bit

fraiseuse *f* milling machine

gant spécial pour soudure à l'arc *m* welding gauntlet

garniture *f* garnet paper

gaz *m* gas

gel thermique anti-chaleur *m* heat gel (gas welding)

générateur *m* rectifier (arc welder)

huile hydraulique *f* hydraulic oil

huile soluble *f* soluble oil

inox *m* stainless steel

fer *m* iron

laiton *m* brass

lame de scie *f* saw blade

lame pour scie à ruban métal *f* band saw blade

lame pour tronçonneuse métal *f* cut-off saw blade

laminé à chaud *m* hot rolled-steel section

laminé à froid *m* cold rolled-steel section

lampe à souder *f* blowtorch

lance de soudage *f* soldering lance

lettres et chiffres à frapper *f* letters and numbers punch set

lime *f* file

lime aiguille *f* needle file

lime carrée *f* square file

lime de précision *f* mini file

lime électrique *f* electric file

lime mi-ronde *f* half-round file
lime plate à main *f* flat file
lime ronde *f* round file
lime tiers point *f* saw file
lunettes de soudage *f*; ~ **de protection** *f* welding goggles
maillet *m*; **masse** *f*; **massette** *f* mallet
maillet à tête plastique *m* plastic-headed mallet (soft metals)
maillet cuivre *m* copper mallet (soft metals)
manchette équipée *f* small bore torch hose (not available in UK)
marteau (*pl* -x) *m* hammer -s
marteau à piquer les soudures *m* chipping hammer (welding)
marteau boule 'anglais'/ 'américain' *m* ball pein hammer
marteau de forgeron *m* blacksmith's hammer
marteau de mécanicien *m* engineer's hammer
marteau postillon *m* sputter hammer (sheet metal work and coppersmithing)
marteau rivoir *m* riveting hammer

masque de soudure arc/MIG *m* arc/MIG welding headshield
mastic soudure à froid universel *m* epoxy resin mastic
métal (*pl* -aux) *m* metal
métal ferreux *m* ferrous metal
métal non-ferreux *m* non-ferrous metal
mètre ruban *m* tape measure
meule *f* grinding disk/grinding wheel
meule à eau *f* whet stone grinder
meule grain fin *f* fine grain grinding wheel
meule gros grain *f* coarse grain grinding wheel
meuleuse *f*; ~ **d'angle** *f* angle grinder
nickel *m* nickel
nickel-argent *m* nickel-silver
nickelage *m* nickel-plating
outils à pastilles carbure démontables *m* lathe cutting tools
outils de soudure *m* welding tools
outils pour tête à aleser *m* reamer tools
oxygène *m* oxygen

papier émeri *m* emery paper

pare flame *f* welding blanket

pâte à polir *f* polishing paste

perceuse *f* drill

perceuse d'établi *f* bench drill

perceuse manuelle *f* manual drill

perceuse sur colonne *f* drill press

pied à coulisse *m* calliper

pied à coulisse digital *m* digital vernier calliper

pied à coulisse vernier *m* vernier calliper

pince *f* pliers

pince à becs coudés éffilés *f* bent nose pliers

pince à becs demi-rond de longueur *f* long nose pliers

pince à becs plats *f* flat long nose pliers

pince à becs ronds *f* round nose pliers

pince coupante de coté de longueur *f* side cutting pliers

pince coupante diagonale *f* side cutters

pince coupante mécanicien *f* mechanic's pincers

pince-étaux bec courts *f* short nose lock grip pliers

pince-étaux bec longs *f* long nose, lock grip pliers

pince MIG *f* MIG pliers

pince multifonctions *f* multi-purpose tool

pince multiprise de longueur *f* water pump pliers

pince multiprise réglable *f* adjustable pipe wrench

pince porte-électrode *f* electrode holder (arc welder)

pince universelle de longueur *f* linesman pliers

pistolet à colle *m* hot glue gun

pistolet à souder *m* electric soldering gun

plate à main *f* flat file

plateau pour disques *m* angle grinder backing pad

pointe à tracer *f* scriber

pointeau *m*; ~ **de précision** *m* centre punch

porte lame *f* mini hacksaw

poste à soudage MIG *m* MIG welder

poste de soudage à l'arc *m* arc welder

poste de soudage à l'arc sans gaz *m* gasless MIG welder

prise de masse *f* earth clamp (arc welder)

propane *m* propane

raccord rapide *m* quickfit connectors (gas welding)

rapporteur d'angle échancré *m* protractor

redresseur à courant continu DC *m* DC inverter (arc welder)

réglet inox flexible *m* flexible stainless steel rule

réglet semi-rigides inox *m* stainless steel rule (graduated both sides)

robinet relais *m* regulating tap

scie *f* saw

scie à métaux *f* hacksaw

scie à métaux monture *f* hacksaw with frame

scie à ruban métal *f* metal cutting band saw

scie circulaire métal *f* circular saw (for metal)

scie sabre *f* sabre saw

scie sauteuse *f* jigsaw

scie sauteuse laser *f* laser jigsaw

scie sauteuse pendulaire *f* pendular jigsaw

socle pour touret *m* pedestal stand grinder

soudure à froid *f* cold soldering

soudure a l'arc *f* arc welding

soudure étain *f* tin solder

soudure gaz *f* gas welding

soudure MIG *f* MIG welding

spray anti-adhérent *m* anti-spatter spray (MIG welding)

stylo soudeur gaz *m* pencil flame torch

support de perçage *m* drill stand

support touret à meuler *m* bench grinder stand

support tronçonnage de meuleuse *m* angle grinder cutting stand

table de soudage *f* welding table

tablier de protection pour soudure à l'arc *m* protective apron

tampon de nettoyage *m* cleaning rag

té à ailes égales *m* equal tee section

tenaille *f*; **pince coupante devant de longeur** *f* pincers

tête *f* cutting nozzle (gas welding)

tête à aleser *f* reamer head (gas welding)

tôle *f* metal sheet

tôle electrozinguée *f*
electroplated zinc sheet

tôle galvanisée *f* galvanised
metal sheet

tôle perforée *f* perforated metal
sheet

torche MIG *f* MIG torch

tour à métaux *m* metal lathe

touret à meuler *m* bench grinder

touret à meuler mixte *m* bench
grinder (with wire wheel)

tournevis lame magnétique *m*
magnetic tip screwdriver

tronçonneuse métal *f* cut-off saw

tube *m* tube

tube carré *m* square hollow
section tube

tube contact vissé *m* MIG
contact tip

tube métal rectangulaire *m*
rectangular hollow section tube

tube rond *m* round metal tube

tuyau *m* welding hose

U à conge *m* U-shaped channel

NOTES

PLOMBERIE & CHAUFFAGE

PLUMBING & HEATING

admission *f* inlet

adoucisseur d'eau *m* water softener

aligner *v* to align

allume-brûleur *m* blowlamp/ blowtorch cup lighter

aluminium *m* aluminium

anti-calcaire magnétique *m* magnetic anti-hardwater device; **~ pour la douche** *m* (for showers); **~ pour machine à laver et lave-vaisselle** *m* (for washing machines/dishwashers)

anti-tartre électronique *f* electronic scale inhibitor

antivibratile *adj* antivibration

applique murale *f* wall plate elbow

assainissement *m* sanitation

bac à poser *m* floor-mounted shower tray

bac dégraisseur *m* grease trap (for drainage system)

baguette de brasure *f* brazing rod

baguette de métal d'apport et étain *f* welding rod

baguette de nettoyage *f* cleaning rod

baignoire *f* bath

baignoire à bulle *f* hydrotherapy bath

baignoir sabot *f* hip-bath

ballon d'eau chaude *m* hot water tank

bidet *m* bidet

billes silico-phosphate anti-calcaire *m* anti-hardwater silico-phosphate balls

bonde *f* plug

bonde à bouchon *f* plughole and plug

bonde de douche *f* shower trap

bouchon fileté *m* access plug

bouchon laiton à souder *m* brass soldered joint stop end

bouteille gaz rechargeable *f* refillable gas bottle

braser *v* to braze; to solder

brûleur à bec plat *m* flat beak soldering nozzle

brûleur à flamme enveloppante *m* enveloping soldering nozzle

brûleur à pointe super fine *m* extra fine point soldering nozzle

brûleur fioul *m* oil burner

brûleur gaz *m* gas burner

brûleur grande flamme *m* large flame soldering nozzle

bulle d'air *f* air bubble

buse de soudage *f* soldering/welding nozzle

butane *m* butane (gas)

cabine de douche *f* shower cabinet

canalisation *f* pipe; pipework

canalisation d'évacuation en plastique *f* plastic waste pipework

canalisation de gaz *f* pipeline (gas)

canalisation en plastique *f* plastic pipework

canalisation vidange *f* waste pipe

canne de vidange extensible *f* extendable washing machine drain hose

caoutchouc *m* rubber

carafe filtrante *f* water filter jug

carneau de chaudière *m* boiler flue

cartouche de rechange *f* replacement water filter cartridge

cartouche filtrante *f* water filter cartridge

cartouche jetable *f* disposable gas bottle

cassette de programmation *f* heating programmer

centrale de traitement d'eau *m* water treatment centre

chalumeau (*pl* -x) *m*; **lampe à souder** *f* blowlamp/blowtorch

chalumeau bi-gaz *f* two gases welding kit

chalumeau monogaz *m* gas blowtorch (butane or propane)

chalumeau soudeur *m* cutting blowtorch (oxy-acetylene or oxy-propane)

chaudière *f* boiler

chaudière au sol *f* floor-standing boiler; **~ avec ballon** *f* (with hot water tank)

chaudière fioul *f* oil boiler; **~ production d'eau chaude par ballon** *f* (with hot water tank)

chaudière gaz *f* gas boiler

chaudière murale *f* wall-mounted boiler; **~ sans ballon** *f* (without hot water tank); **~ avec ballon** *f* (with hot water tank)

chauffage *m* heating

chauffage au fioul *m* oil heating

chauffage au gaz *m* gas heating

chauffage centrale *m* central heating

chauffage d'appoint *m* back-up heating

chauffe-eau *m* water heater

chauffe-eau électrique *m* electric water heater (equiv. immersion heater)

chauffe-eau gaz instantané *m* instantaneous gas water heater

chauffe-eau solaire *m* solar water heater

chauffer *v* to heat

cheminée *f* flue

circulateur trois vitesse *f* three-speed circulating pump

citerne *f* cistern

clapet anti-pollution *m* anti-pollution valve

clé *f* wrench; spanner *(see also: pince)*

clé à chaine *f* chain wrench

clé à molette *f* adjustable wrench; ~ spanner

clé anglaise *f* monkey wrench

clé de montage de radiateur *f* radiator head tool

clé lavabo *f* basin wrench

clé purgeur à radiateur *f* radiator bleed key

clé Stillson *f* Stillson wrench

clé Suédoise *f* plumber's wrench

clé Suédoise *f*; **serre-tubes Suédoise** *f* plumber's pliers; tube tightening pliers

colle PVC *f* PVC solvent-weld adhesive

collet *m* flange

collier *m* hose clip

collier à crémaillère *m* ratcheted hose clip

collier à crémaillère à vis *m* fixed bridge clamp

collier simple *m* pipe clip

colmater *v* to seal off

compteur *m* meter

compteur d'eau froide *m* water meter

compteur de volume *m* volume meter

conduit fumée *f* smoke pipe

conduite *f* duct

contre-courant *m* counterflow

corroder *v* to corrode

corrosion *f* corrosion

coude à joint *m* conversion bend

coude de renvoi *m* S-bend

coude de tube *m* pipe bend

coude en U *m* U-bend

coulisse *f* straight connector

coupe-tube *f* tube cutter; pipe cutter

coupe-tube cuivre *f* copper pipe cutter

cuivre recuit (en couronne) *m* microbore tube (in coil)

cuvette *f* toilet bowl; basin; bowl

cylindre *m* cylinder

débordement *m* overflow

décharge *f* outlet

désinfectant pour adoucisseurs *m* water softener disinfectant

douche *f* shower

douchette *f* shower rose

déboucheur *m* drain clearing tool

déboucheur à piston *m* piston drain clearing tool

déboucheur à tambour *m* spool drain clearing tool

déboucheur fléxible à manivele *m*; **~ à crampons** *m* cranked spring drain clearing tool

débrancher *v* to disconnect

décapant *m* abrasive agent

décharge *f* discharge

décrasser *v* to scour

désinfectant pour adoucisseurs *m* water softener disinfectant

désinfection *f* disinfection

détecteur de fuites *m* leak detector

détendeur *m* gas regulator; pressure reducing valve

eau *f* water

eau buvable *f* drinking water

eaux d'égout brutes *fpl* raw sewage

eaux usées *fpl* sewage

écrêteur *m* pressure regulator

égout *m* drain; sewer

égoutter *v* to drip

embout alimentation en 'Y' *m* Y piece washing machine drain hose

emporte-pièce *m* hole-making punch

encroûtement *m* scale deposit

entrée *f* inlet

épuration *f* purification

épurer *v* to purge; to purify

étanchéité *f* watertight

évier *m* sink

fil d'étanchéité bobine *m* pipe seal cord

fil de soudure *m*; ~ **d'étain à braser** *m* solder; solder wire

filtrante de l'eau *f* water filter

filtre anti-tartre pour machine à laver *m* washing machine limescale filter

flux décapant *m* flux

fosse d'aisances *f* cesspool

fosse septique *f*; ~ **'toutes eaux'** *f* septic tank

fuite *f* leak; leakage

gaine *f* conduit

galvaniser *v* to galvanise

gaz *m* gas

gaz naturel *m* natural gas

grille du filtre *f* filter mesh

gouttière *f* gutter

groupe de sécurité *m* security valves

imperméable *adj* impermeable

incrustations *fpl* scale

isolation *f* insulation

isoler *v* to insulate

joint *m* connector

joint caoutchouc serrage manuel *m* rubber washer (manual tightening)

joint CSC pour eau chaude *m* CSC washer (hot water)

joint d'étanchéité *m* gasket; seal

joint de raccord *m* washer

joint de robinet *m* tap washer

joint fibre pour eau froide *m* fibre washer (cold water)

kit bypass pour filtre *m* water filter bypass system kit

kit de raccordement universel pour chaudière *m* boiler connection kit

kit robinet et filter *m* tap kit and filter

lance de soudage *f* soldering lance

lavabo *m*; **lave-mains** *m*; **vasque** *f* (wash)basin

lime *f* file

lunettes de soudage *fpl* welding goggles

machine à laver *f* washing machine

malette cintreuse *f*; **pince à cintrer** *f* pipe bending tool

manchette réparation *f* straight male to female connector

manchon cuivre à souder *m* straight soldered joint

manchon sans lèvre *m* straight connector without lip

manomètre *m* manometer

mastique à réparer les fuites *m* leak repair mastic

mélangeur *m*; **mitigeur** *m* mixer tap

mitigeur thermostatique *m* tap with temperature control

molette pour coupe-tube cuivre *f* replacement pipe cutter blade

nettoyer *v* to clean

neutraliseur de calcaire *f* hard water neutraliser

niveau de l'eau *m* water level

outil universel pour emboîtement *m* socket forming tool

pare-douche *m* shower screen

pare-flamme *m* welding blanket

pastilles de sel pour adoucisseur d'eau *f* water softener salt tablets

pince *f* pliers *(see also: clé)*

pince à siphon *f*; **~ griptou** *f* adjustable wide jaw pliers

plomb *m* plumbline

plomber *v* to plumb

plomberie *f* plumber's workshop; plumbing

poche d'air *f* air pocket

pompe à chaleur *f* heat pump

pompe à vide *f* drain clearing pump

pompe de circulation *f*

pompe de relevage *f* macerator

pompe électrique *f* electric pump

poste à souder *f* welding kit

poudre détartrante et dégraissante pour lave-linge et lave-vaisselle *f* de-limescaling powder for washing machines and dishwashers

pression *f* pressure

prise de vidange universel *m* washing machine waste outlet kit

propane *m* propane (gas)

purgeur à bec *m*; **~ équerre** *m* draincock

purgeur automatique pour radiateur *m* automatic radiator bleed valve

purgeur pour radiateur *m* radiator bleed valve

raccord à olive *m* brass compression joint with olive

raccord coude cuivre à souder *m* soldered elbow joint

raccord courbe cuivre à souder *m* soldered angle joint

raccord cuivre *m* copper joint

raccord cuivre à souder *m* copper soldered joint (capillary fitting)

raccord d'évacuation souple *m* flexible waste pipe

raccord sortie lavabo *m* washbasin waste pipe connector

raccord té cuivre à souder *m* soldered tee joint

raccord té cuivre à souder égal *m* soldered equal tee joint

raccord té cuivre à souder réduction *m* soldered reducing tee joint

raccord tourant bicone *m* tap connector

raccord vidange *m* waste pipe connector

radiateur *m* radiator

radiateur à eau *m* water-filled radiator

radiateur sèche-serviette *m* towel radiator

receveur à encaster *m* inset shower tray

receveur de douche *m* shower tray

receveur surélevé *m* raised shower tray

réchauffeur *m* heater

réducteur de pression *m* pressure reducer

réducteur de pression spécial chauffe-eau *m* water heater pressure reducer

réduction *f*; **manchon dilation** *m* reducing connector

réduction excentrée *f* off-centre reducing connector

regard *m* manhole

regard de branchement pour eaux pluviales *m* rainwater gully

régler *v* to regulate

régulateur *m* regulator

réservoir *m* reservoir

réservoir d'eau *m* water butt

ressort à cintrer *m* pipe bending spring

robinet *m* tap; (nearest equivalent) bibcock

robinet à boisseau *m* cock

robinet à commande unique *m* separate control tap

robinet autoperceur *m* self-cutting tap

robinet d'arrêt *m* stoptap; stopcock

robinet d'arrêt à raccord sans purge *m* stoptap without drain valve

robinet d'arrêt avec purge *m* stoptap with drain valve

robinet de puisage *m* stoptap with hose connector

robinet de radiateur *m* radiator tap

robinet de radiateur à tête thermostatique *m* thermostatic radiator valve

robinet extérieur *m* outside tap

robinet manette crosillon *m* cross-head tap

robinet pousser/tourner *m* push and turn gas tap

robinet poussoir *m* push tap

robinet relais gaz *m* gas regulating tap

robinetterie *f* taps

rodoir *m* tap reseating tool

rosace conique *f* conical back plate pipe clip

rosace plate *f* flat back plate pipe clip

ruban caoutchouc pour colmatage *m* rubber pipe sealing tape

ruban Téflon d'étanchéité *m* PTFE joint sealing tape

sanitaire *adj* sanitary

scie à métaux *f* hacksaw

sédiment *m* sediment

selle tuyau *f* soil pipe saddle

sel régénérant pour adoucisseur d'eau *m* water softener regenerating salt

serre-tubes *m* pipe wrench

siphon *m* siphon

siphon *m* (waste) trap

siphon avec tube droit *m* upstand

siphon canal net *m*; **siphon à culot** *m* bottle trap

siphon évier multi-positions *m* multi-position sink trap

siphon évier *m*; **prise machine à laver** *m* sink/washing machine trap

siphon gain de place lavabo/ bidet *m* washbasin/bidet waste trap

soudage *m*; **soudure** *f*; **soudure à la flame** *f* soldering

souder *v* to solder; to weld

soudure autogène *f*; **~ à la flame** *f* welding

soupape *f* valve

système de drainage *m* drainage system

système de vidange *m* waste outlet system

système du tout à l'égout *m* sewage system

tampon de nettoyage *m* cleaning rag

tampon de réduction *m* waste to soil pipe adapter

tampon double *m* double waste to soil pipe adapter

té égal *m* equal tee connector

té pied biche *m* tee piece

télécommande téléphonique vocale *f* telephone remote control (heating control)

tête de filère *f* die head

tête de robinet *f* tap head

thermostat *m* thermostat

thermostat de haute précision *m* high precision thermostat

thermostat électronique *m* electronic thermostat

thermostat électronique programmable radio/tél *m* radio/telephone control thermostat

thermostat mécanique *m* mechanical thermostat

thermostat programmable *m* programmable thermostat

traitement de l'eau *m* water treatment

trop-plein *m* overflow

tube de cuivre *m*; **~ cuivre écroui** *m*; **tuyau de cuivre** *m* copper tube

tube en PVC-C *m* CPVC tube

tubulure *f* piping

tuyau *m* pipe; welding hose

tuyau à gaz *m* gas pipe

tuyau cuivre *m* copper pipe

tuyau d'arrosage *m* hosepipe

tuyau d'écoulement *m* drainpipe

tuyau d'entrée *m* inlet pipe

tuyau de trop-plein *m* overflow pipe

tuyau flexible d'alimentation souple *m* hand-bendable pipe

tuyau flexible pour gaz naturel *m* flexible gas pipe (natural gas)

tuyau polyethylène eau potable *m* MDPE blue water pipe

tuyau PVC *m* PVC pipe (plastic, polyvinylchloride)

robinet d'arrêt *m* stopcock

robinet extérieur *m* outside tap

unité de traitement d'eau *m*
water treatment unit

vanne *f* ball valve

vanne à passage intégral *f*
through ball valve

vanne à sphère *f* tap ball
valve; **~ puisage** (with hose
connector); **~ avec purges**
(with purge); **~ raccords
bicônes** *f* T-type ball valve

vanne d'arrêt *f* stopvalve

vanne papillon *f* ball valve with
butterfly tap

vanne pour compteur *f* ball
valve (alongside meter)

vase d'expansion sanitaire *f*
expansion bottle

ventouse *f* air vent

vidanger *v* to drain off

vider *v* to drain

WC *mpl*; **vécés** *mpl* toilet

NOTES

PROPRIETE

PROPERTY

HOUSES
BUILDINGS
ROOMS
LANDSCAPE
LEGAL
PURCHASE

à louer *adj* for rent

à vendre *adj* for sale

abri; ~ voiture *m* carport

accidenté *adj* hilly

achat de maison et terrain *m*
house and land purchase

acheteur -euse *mf* buyer;
purchaser

acompte *m* deposit

acte d'achat *m* conveyance of land
transfer; deed of sale *(see also: acte
de vente)*

acte de décès *m* death certificate

acte de naissance *m* birth
certificate

acte de vente *m*; **~ authentique
de vente** *m* deed of sale *(see also:
acte d'achat)*

acte notarié *m* property deed

acte sous seing privé *m* private
pre-sale agreement

arrhes *fpl* advance deposit on
purchase

atelier *m* workshop

attestation *f* attestation; affidavit

attestation d'acquisition *f*
notarial certificate (confirming
completion of property
purchase)

bail *m* lease to tenant

barrière *f*; **cloture** *f* fence

bastide *f* Provençal country
house

bergerie *f* sheep farm

bibliothèque *f* library

bon pour achat *expr* good for
acquisition (phrase written
accompanying signature of
contract) *(see also: lu et approuvé)*

buanderie *f* laundry/utility
room

bungalow *m* bungalow

bureau *m* office

cadastre *m* land registry

**caisse des dépots et
consignations** *f* non-interest
accruing bank account (used by
notaire for deposits)

carte de séjour *f*; **permis de
séjour** *m* residency permit
(discontinued)

cave *f* cellar

certificat d'urbanisme *m*
certificate equivalent to a local
authority search

chai *m* wine warehouse

chambre *f* bedroom

champ *m* field

chaumière *f* thatched cottage

chemin *m* path

clause pénale *f* penalty clause

clause suspensive *f* let-out
  clause

colline *f* hill

comble *m* attic

compromis de vente *m*
  purchase agreement; contract
  of sale

conditions suspensives *fpl*
  conditional terms in a pre-sale
  agreement

conservation des hypothèques
  f mortgage/land registry

contrat de réservation *m*;
  contrat préliminaire *m*
  purchase contract

copropriété *f* co-ownership

cottage *m* cottage

cuisine *f* kitchen

débarras *m* junk room

dépendance *f* outbuilding; part
  of a farm

droit de préemption *m* pre-
  emptive right (to acquire
  property instead of purchaser)

droit de succession/donation
  m inheritance/gift tax

droits d'enregistrement
  m registration of title of
  ownership

écurie *f* stable (for horse)

émoluments *m* notary's scale of
  charges

étable *f* cowshed; cattleshed;
  byre

étang *m* pond

états des lieux *m* schedule
  of condition/delapidations
  (beginning or end of a lease)

expédition *f* certified copy of
  notarial document

extrait d'acte de mariage *m*
  marriage certificate

ferme *f* farmhouse

fermette *f* small farm; country/
  weekend cottage

fonds de roulement *m* funds
  supplied by flat-owners to
  meet unexpected liabilities

fossé *m* ditch

frais de notaire *mpl* sum
  to be paid to the notary
  (including sale price, notary's
  fee, registration duty, land
  registration duty and other
  charges)

garage *m* garage

garde-manger *m* larder

gentilhommière *f* country
  manor house

grange *f* barn

grenier *m* attic; granary

hectare *m* approx. 2½ acres

hypothèque *f* mortgage in which property is used as loan security

indivision *f* joint ownership

inondations *fpl* flooding

jouissance *f* life interest

kilomètre carré *m* square kilometre

limite du terrain *f* boundary

location *f* rental; lease

loi scrivener *f* law protecting borrowers (from French lenders and sellers on French property purchases)

longère *f* Breton stone-built farmhouse; long house

lot *m* land registry plot applied in an apartment block

lotissement *m* housing estate; plot of land

lu et approuvé *expr* read and approved (phrase written accompanying signature of contract) *(see also: bon pour achat)*

maison *f* house; home; abode; residence

maison bourgeoise *f* mansion

maison d'amis *f* weekend house

maison de banlieue *f* suburban house

maison de campagne *f* country house

maison de chasse *f* hunting lodge

maison d'habitation *f* dwelling house

maison de maître *f* gentleman's house

maison de plaisance *f* weekend/holiday house

maison de rapport *f* apartment block; block of flats

maison de repos *f*; ~ **de convalescence** *f* rest home; convalescent home

maison de retraite *f* retirement home

maison de ville *f* town house

maison meublée *f* furnished apartment

maison paysanne *f* farmhouse

maisonette *f* small house; cottage

maisonette de garde-barrière *f* level-crossing keeper's cottage

maisons doubles *fpl* semi-detached houses

maisonette du garde *f* gatekeeper's lodge

mandat de recherche *m* agreement authorising estate agent to search for property

mandat de vente *m* agreement to sell

marais *m* marshland

mas *m* Provençal farmhouse (low, L-shaped)

monument historique *m* listed building

niveau de la mer *m* sea level

nue-propriété *f* ownership without usufruct (in which purchaser has no occupational rights over a property until death or prior surrender of life tenant)

offre d'achat *f*; **offer de vente** *f* non-binding offer to buy or sell property

paiement comptant *m* cash payment

pailler *m* barn for straw

parties communes *fpl* communal parts of a building

parties privatives *fpl* parts of a building restricted solely to use of owner

pavillon *m* bungalow

pente *f* slope

permis de construire *m* planning permission

pigeonnier *m* pigeon tower

piquet de clôture *f* fence post

plan de financement *m* financing scheme

plus-value *f* capital gains tax

porcherie *f* pigsty

poteau télégraphique *m* telegraph pole

procuration *f* power of attorney

propriétaire *mf* landowner

pylône *m* pylon

reçu *m* receipt

résidence secondaire *f* weekend/holiday house

résiliation *f* cancellation of a contract

salle à manger *f* dining room

salle de bain *f* bathroom

salle de séjour *f* family room

salon *m* living room

source *f* spring

sous-sol *m* basement

système d'assainissement *f* drainage

taillis *m* copse

tantième *m* proportion
  of communal parts of a
  co-ownership with other
  apartment owners
terrain à bâtir *m* building land
terrain constructible *m* land
  designated for building
testament *m* will
timbre fiscal *f* revenue stamp
tontine *f* joint ownership
vendeur -euse *mf* vendor; seller
vente aux enchères *f* auction
véranda *f* conservatory
vestibule *m* entrance hall

NOTES

METIERS

TRADES

agent d'assurance *m* insurance
agent

agent immobilier *m* estate
agent

agriculteur -trice *mf* farmer

ambulancier -ère *mf*
ambulance driver

architecte *mf* architect

arpenteur -euse *mf* surveyor
(see also: géomètre)

artisan -e *mf* craftsman/woman

avocat -e *mf* lawyer

bricoleur -euse *mf* handyman/
woman

cariste *m* quarryman

charpentier *m* carpenter

chauffagiste *m* heating
specialist

constructeur *m* builder

contremaître -esse *mf*; **maître
d'oeuvre** *m* foreman/woman

couvreur *m* roofer

déménageur *m* removal
company

dessinateur -trice *mf*
draughtsman/woman

docteur *m* doctor

ébéniste *mf* cabinet maker

électricien *m* electrician

éleveur *m* cattleman

expert-comptable *m* chartered
accountant

expert-conseil *m* consultant

expert foncier *m* expert
(architect or other, licensed
to check state and value of
property)

expert immobilier *m*
diagnostic professional (e.g.
testing for lead and asbestos)

ferronnier -ière *mf* iron
craftsman/woman

forgeron *m* blacksmith

garagiste *mf* mechanic/service
station worker

géomètre *mf* surveyor *(see also:
arpenteur -euse)*

gendarme *m* police officer

horticulteur -trice *mf*
horticulturist

informaticien -enne *mf*;
informatique *f* computer
specialist

jardinier -ière *mf* gardener

maçon *m* bricklayer

mains-d'oeuvre *m* workforce

maraîcher -ère *mf* market
gardener

marchand -e *mf* shopkeeper;
tradesman/woman

marchand -e de biens *mf* property dealer

medécin *m* medical doctor

menuisier *m* joiner

métreur -euse *mf* quantity surveyor; supervisor

mutuelle *f* mutual insurance company

notaire *m* notary

officier de police *m* police officer *(see also: policier)*

ouvrier -ière *mf* workman/ worker

paysagiste *mf* landscape gardener

peintre *m* painter

pépiniériste *mf* nurseryman

plâtrier *m* plasterer

plombier *m* plumber

plombier-zinguer *m* zinc- roofer

policier *m* policeman *(see also: officier de police)*

pompier *m*; **sapeur-pompier** *m* fireman

quincaillier -ière *mf* hardware merchant

ramoneur *m* chimneysweep

secrétaire *mf* secretary

serrurier -ière *mf* locksmith

tapissier -ière *mf* upholsterer

tapissier décorateur *m* interior decorator

terrassier -ière *mf* landscape labourer

traiteur *m* caterer

travailleur -euse *mf* labourer

vétérinaire *mf* veterinarian

vidangeur *m* cesspool cleaner

vitrier *m* glazier

NOTES

LES NOMBRES

NUMBERS

NUMBERS
FRACTIONS
DECIMALS
PERCENTAGES

0 zéro nought

1 un (une) one

2 deux two

3 trois three

4 quatre four

5 cinq five

6 six six

7 sept seven

8 huit eight

9 neuf nine

10 dix ten

11 onze eleven

12 douze twelve

13 treize thirteen

14 quatorze fourteen

15 quinze fifteen

16 seize sixteen

17 dix-sept seventeen

18 dix-huit eighteen

19 dix-neuf nineteen

20 vingt twenty

21 vingt et un (une) twenty-one

22 vingt-deux twenty-two

23 vingt-trois twenty-three

24 vingt-quatre twenty-four

25 vingt-cinq twenty-five

26 vingt-six twenty-six

27 vingt-sept twenty-seven

28 vingt-huit twenty-eight

29 vingt-neuf twenty-nine

30 trente thirty

40 quarante forty

50 cinquante fifty

60 soixante sixty

70 soixante-dix seventy

71 soixante et onze seventy-one

72 soixante-douze seventy-two

80 quatre-vingts eighty

81 quatre-vingt-un (une) eighty-one

90 quatre-vingt-dix ninety

91 quatre-vingt-onze ninety-one

100 cent a hundred

101 cent un a hundred and one

200 deux cents two hundred

201 deux cent un (une) two hundred and one

300 trois cents three hundred

1,000 mille a thousand

1,000,000 un million a million

1er premier -ière 1st first

2e / 2ème deuxième 2nd second

3e / 3ème troisième 3rd third

4e / 4ème quatrième 4th fourth

5e / 5ème cinquième 5th fifth

6e / 6ème sixième 6th sixth

7e / 7ème septième 7th seventh

8e / 8ème huitième 8th eighth

9e / 9ème neuvième 9th ninth

10e / 10ème dixième 10th tenth

11e / 11ème onzième 11th eleventh

12e / 12ème douzième 12th twelfth

13e / 13ème treizième 13th thirteenth

14e / 14ème quatorzième 14th fourteenth

15e / 15ème quinzième 15th fifteenth

16e / 16ème seizième 16th sixteenth

17e / 17ème dix-septième 17th seventeenth

18e / 18ème dix-huitième 18th eighteenth

19e / 19ème dix-neuvième 19th nineteenth

20e / 20ème vingtième 20th twentieth

21e / 21ème vingt-et-unième 21st twenty-first

30e / 30ème trentième 30th thirtieth

100e / 100ème centième 100th hundredth

101e / 101ème cent-unième 101st hundred-and-first

1,000^e / 1,000^{ème} millième 1,000th thousandth

LES FRACTIONS FRACTIONS

un demi a half

un tiers a third

deux tiers two-thirds

un quart a quarter

un cinquième a fifth

LES DECIMAUX DECIMALS

0,5 zéro virgule cinq 0.5 nought point five

POURCENTAGE PERCENTAGES

5% cinq pour cent 5% five per cent

100% cent pour cent 100% one hundred per cent

NOTES

Letter	French pronunciation
a	ah
b	bay
c	say
d	day
e	euh
f	effe
g	jhay
h	ashe
i	ee
j	jhi
k	kah
l	elle
m	emme
n	enne
o	oh
p	pay
q	ku
r	erre
s	esse
t	tay
u	oo
v	vay
w	doo-bleuh-vay
x	eeks
y	ee grec
z	zed

USEFUL PHRASES

**I've got an emergency. Can you send
someone out immediately?**

J'ai une urgence. Pourriez-vous envoyer quelqu'un immédiatement?

I would like to order/buy…

Je voudrais ordonner/acheter…

Do you stock…

Est-ce que vous avez…/Avez-vous…

Can you give me a quote for…

Pourriez-vous me donner un devis pour…

I'd like to make an appointment/organise a survey/meeting.

Je voudrais prendre rendez-vous/organiser
une inspection/une rencontre.

I would like to enquire about…

Je voudrais me renseigner sur…

I would like some information about…

Je voudrais des renseignements sur…

When can you come?

Quand est-ce que vous pouvez venir?

When will you be able to finish…?

Quand est-ce que vous pourrez finir/terminer…?

Is there someone you can recommend?

Pouvez-vous recommander quelqu'un? / Est-ce
que vous pouvez recommander quelqu'un?

Also by the author

Richard Wiles

Bon Courage!

A French renovation in rural Limousin

Bon Courage!

A French Renovation in Rural Limousin

Richard Wiles

£7.99 Pb

1 84024 360 0

ISBN 13: 978 1 84024 360 4

A dilapidated, rat-infested stone barn set amidst thirteen acres of unkempt pasture and overgrown woodland might not be many people's vision of a potential dream home. But for English couple Richard and his wife Al, the cavernous, oak-beamed building in a sleepy hamlet in the Limousin region of France is perfect.

Tussles with French bureaucracy allied with fierce storms that wreak havoc on the property do little to dampen their resolve as they immerse themselves in the *calme* of this quiet corner of France, dreaming of taking trips in Richard's hot-air balloon and starting their very own llama farm.

'This book will trigger dreams... humorously highlights the obstacles they had to overcome to fulfil their dream'

Country House and Home

'...hilarious, farcical, frustrating and poignant, the writing of the ever-optimistic Richard captures all that is French'

The Book Place

Richard Wiles

Bonne Chance!

Building a Life in Rural France

'France doesn't get any more profonde than this'
Rupert Wright

Bonne Chance!

Building a Life in Rural France

Richard Wiles

£7.99 Pb

1 84024 493 3

ISBN 13: 978 1 84024 493 9

Deep in the Limousin countryside, Richard Wiles bought his dream home. But little did he expect to be living full time in the dilapidated farmhouse and struggling to finish the conversion during the insect plagues of summer and the harsh blizzards of winter.

Watched by his bemused neighbours, Richard pursued his more unusual dreams of raising llamas, hot-air ballooning and marathon running whilst trying to keep the roof over his head. Told with unfailing humour and optimism, this is a unique tale of overcoming the challenges of building a home, and a life, in France.

'France doesn't get any more *profonde* than this'

Rupert Wright

Extract from
Bon Courage!

Chapter Three

Le Mas Mauvis

As we drove down the rutted track that led to the property we were assailed by the sound of dogs barking. Lots of dogs barking. Or perhaps 'howling' would be a more appropriate word. On our right was an assortment of dilapidated buildings. There was a simple cottage, the windows of which were badly rotten and glazed with polythene and fronds of ivy instead of glass, with a substantial tree sprouting jauntily from the base of its front wall. There was also an attached barn with an undulating clay-tiled roof and a gaping cart entrance, its oak doors hanging obliquely from their hinges. Beyond that was a row of two modest barns connected to a much larger stone *grange* with an open-fronted hangar attached to its other side, intended for the storage of hay bales or machinery. Half-hidden behind the barns and the cottage we could just glimpse another small cottage with exposed brick window reveals. Assorted rusty farm machinery and huge plastic bags of white fertiliser littered the ground around the buildings, while the dismembered corpses of unidentifiable animals (fowl apparently, judging by the presence of feathers) lay scattered around. Scrawny chickens pecked at the corpses, having seemingly turned to cannibalism through the effects of starvation.

As we climbed out of the car we were startled by the lithe figure of a black and white border collie, which shot silently from its hiding place beneath an ancient piece of machinery and began to circle around our legs, ears flat against its head, its pointed jaws snapping menacingly at our heels as if it was rounding up a flock of wayward sheep. The dog's nimbleness was not in the least compromised by the fact that it possessed only three legs: two at the back and one at the front. As the tripedal animal wove between us, the odour of manure that clung to its sleek fur told us that this creature was clearly not a cosseted pet but a working cow dog.

The front door of the little house on the opposite side of the track creaked open and a broad-shouldered man with a thatch of black hair emerged, dressed in oil-stained denim jeans and a shirt open to the chest. '*Allez! Allez!*' he snapped at the dog. The animal scuttled back under its hiding place and peered out at us, panting furiously and quivering with nervous excitement.

Had the man's skin been green rather than sun-bronzed, he could easily have been the body double for The Incredible Hulk. In a stance presumably borne of a lifetime of wrestling cows to the ground and hogtying them, his arms were held bowed at his sides and he walked with his head down. He appeared about to charge and fell us with a rugby tackle. (Indeed, as we learned later, the young man had toyed with a career as a rugby player, but opted for farming.) This giant swaggered over and, introduced by Hero as Monsieur Jérôme L'Heureux, the owner of the farm, gripped our hands in a greeting that left my fingers throbbing. After various formalities were exchanged between Hero and the burly farmer, our redheaded guide turned to us and said: 'Would you like to have a look around, then?'

'Yes. But which property is for sale, exactly?' I queried naively, puzzled by the motley collection of buildings ranged before us.

'All of it,' came Hero's reply.

'All of it?' Al and I squeakily chirped in unison, consulting the agent's details again in disbelief, and homing in on the price:

150,000 francs, including *notaire*'s fees, government taxes and the agent's fee. That equated to about £15,000 at the prevailing exchange rate. For an entire farm? Surely not!

'*Tous les bâtiments*,' said the farmer, pointing in turn at each of the buildings. He showed us around the first house and its attached barn (which contained an ancient, rusting blue Citroën and a splendid antique two-wheeled charabanc), pointing out features he considered selling points sure to impress us, such as the shallow stone sink in a recess near the door of the house and an ancient bread oven, housed in a lobby behind a room crammed with huge fuel storage tanks, the floor slick with oil. Judging by its advanced state of decay, however, the dome-shaped oven, set within a wall rendered with strawed mud, had not yielded a single baguette for many a year. The back elevation of the cottage was clad with mature ivy, the tendrils of which had wormed their way into the joints between the stones, dislodging many.

The small detached cottage that nestled between the first house and the row of barns was undeniably quaint and characterful. Its front façade – with brick reveals typical of the region – had no outlook, facing as it did the back of one of the barns. It comprised two rooms with a beaten earth floor pitted with rat holes, leading from a central front door, and at the rear a corrugated-tin-roofed extension housing four pigpens, *sans cochons*, with a stone-walled terrace beyond. The traditional casement window frames on the front of the house were rotten, the glass long since replaced with plastic, which had discoloured nicotine yellow after prolonged exposure to the sun. Louvre shutters hung at jaunty angles at each side of the windows, held back against the wall with traditional metal *tête bergère*: retainers in the shape of a shepherd's head. Tiny windows with brick reveals peeped from beneath the verge of the tiled roof, which itself was inlaid with two rows of half-round tiles separated by flat tiles as decoration.

[...] The main barn was outwardly nothing more than a utilitarian stone structure: not a period building, being constructed in the early 1900s, yet built in a style that has been traditional in this area of France for hundreds of years. Its symmetry gave it an air of grace and elegance that belied its intended function. Stout and sturdy walls of sand-coloured stone bonded with nothing more than mud, although mortar-pointed, measured over a metre thick; its steeply pitched apex roof was clad on the front elevation with grey *ardoises*, slates, and on the rear with russet-coloured clay tiles. In the middle of the front façade of the barn was a broad, arched access hole large enough to swallow a fully-laden cart. Stout oak doors at each side folded back against the front wall. The pegged joints of the barn doors had sagged and the cladding was rotten at the base. At each side of the barn entrance were two smaller ancillary doorways with stone lintels and weathered oak plank doors through which the animals could pass. On the top floor, original oak shutters – grainy planks bolted to a ledged-and-braced frame – flanked a pair of side openings measuring just over a metre wide by nearly two metres in height. More like doors than windows, these openings were evidently intended for the loading and unloading of materials. A central, broader opening about two metres square and arched with a soldier course of red bricks was fitted with inward-opening shutters, and in its heyday would perhaps have been fitted with a hoist to haul sacks of grain from a wagon to the upper floor for conversion into meal.

www.summersdale.com